Dear Melody

EXPERIENCING
THE
FATHER'S
Embrace

Happy Birthday

With His Love

Rose

Jan 31.

JACK FROST

Charisma
HOUSE

EXPERIENCING THE FATHER'S EMBRACE by Jack Frost
Published by Charisma House
A part of Strang Communications Company
600 Rinehart Road
Lake Mary, Florida 32746
www.charismahouse.com

Unless otherwise noted, all Scripture quotations are from the New American Standard Bible. Copyright © 1960, 1962, 1963, 1968, 1971, 1972, 1973, 1975, 1977 by the Lockman Foundation. Used by permission. (www.Lockman.org)

Scripture quotations marked AMP are from the Amplified Bible. Old Testament copyright © 1965, 1987 by the Zondervan Corporation. The Amplified New Testament copyright © 1954, 1958, 1987 by the Lockman Foundation. Used by permission.

Scripture quotations marked NKJV are from the New King James Version of the Bible. Copyright © 1979, 1980, 1982 by Thomas Nelson, Inc., publishers. Used by permission.

Scripture quotations marked THE MESSAGE are from *The Message*, copyright © 1993, 1994, 1995. Used by permission of NavPress Publishing Group.

Cover design by Karen Gonsalves

Library of Congress Cataloging-in-Publication Data
Frost, Jack, 1952-
Experiencing the Father's embrace / by Jack Frost.
p. cm.
Includes bibliographical references.
ISBN 0-88419-845-6 (trade paper)

1. God—Love. 2. Love—Religious aspects—Christianity. I. Title.
BT140 .F76 2002
231'.6—dc21
2002011524

02 03 04 05 — 8 7 6 5 4 3 2 1
Printed in the United States of America

Dedicated to my wife, Trisha, whose patience
with me modeled to me God's grace!

It was her love that brought to me a rest,
A love that my pain has put to the test.
What pain can hold back such a love as ours,
Not shame, not fear, not even wounded hearts.
Certainly her love must come from above,
How else could we know such a wondrous love!

Acknowledgments

I would like to thank the many people who have impacted my life and, directly or indirectly, influenced the writing of this book.

I thank Lee Grady, who was so impacted by the message of the Father's unconditional love that he personally pursued this project with the desire to be the chief editor. Thank you goes also to Christy Sterner for helping Lee with the writing. They were the wordsmiths that waded through so much of my teaching, thoughts and experiences and helped put them in print so that you, the reader, may experience the Father's embrace.

There were two very special men who helped bring the personal, experiential revelation of the Father's love to my own heart. In so doing, they have become my friends. I am indebted to the late Jack Winter for his book *The Homecoming* and for his personal mentoring and impartation of the message to me. I also thank Ed Piorek for his book *The Father Loves You* and for his intellectual ability to simplify the theology and ministry of the Father's love.

I thank John and Carol Arnott for the humility and rest that I saw in their life and ministry when I first encountered them in 1995. Their very presence convicted me of my pride and aggressive striving. Their message on Law and Grace helped to set me free from the love of law and to lead me into a higher way, the way of grace and God's love. My family and I are ever indebted to their friendship and the revelation that they imparted to us.

I am so thankful for James Jordan, whose own experiences and friendship have helped bring me out of feeling like a spiritual orphan and into living life like a favored son. His wife, Denise, brought to me the revelation of the mother heart of Father God and helped me enter into deeper fellowship with His affectionate, comforting and nurturing heart.

I am so thankful for the ministry of John and Paula Sandford and Elijah House. Without them in our early years of ministry, my wife and I may never have made it through all the judgment, pain and disappointments that we carried. Their revelation of Bitter Root Judgment and Expectations (ungodly beliefs) and the repentance that I began walking out daily was foundational to my experiencing the Father's embrace.

I thank my staff and ministry team at Shiloh Place Ministries. I have rarely seen such a group of faithful, loyal and committed people. God has surrounded my wife and me with people in whom we can entrust our life and ministry. They have selflessly given themselves to seeing the message of the Father's love taken to the nations of the earth.

Without pastoral leaders to hold us accountable, my wife and I would have probably self-destructed years ago. I must thank Pastor Phillip and Lynn Miles for watching over our souls since 1986 and for always valuing and believing in us even when we lost faith in ourselves. I thank Pastor Chip and Coleen Judd for sticking it out with us and for the great wisdom that they have spoken into our life and ministry over the years. It has been these couples' love, friendship and willingness to ask the hard questions and to speak the truth in love that have helped us to mature to the point that this book is possible. They helped us see God's perspective during each point of change and transition that we were in.

My heartfelt gratitude goes to Cape and Brenda Grice, my brother and sister-in-law, whose continual prayers helped sustain my wife and me through the years. In 1979, they gave me *The Living Bible*, which drew me close to God's love.

Contents

SECTION ONE
A REVELATION OF THE FATHER'S LOVE

SECTION TWO
HINDRANCES TO EXPERIENCING THE FATHER'S LOVE

SECTION THREE
PROCESSING THE FATHER'S LOVE

Foreword

I believe with all my heart that the message of the Father's love is one of the most important messages to be shared in today's world. It is central to one's relationship with God. It is central to one's relationships with others. And it has the power to unlock healing and restoration like the world has never seen. The message is a simple one, and yet to walk in the day-to-day experience of the Father's unconditional love and acceptance is something few people truly know.

I have met people all over the world who have exhausted themselves trying to find real love and acceptance. Many of us have experienced the peace and rest that come from being in God's presence, and yet we can still struggle to walk in this experience on an ongoing basis. And so we perform and compete, trying to earn a place and be a success. We can be subtly motivated by fear and end up controlling and manipulating those around us. Even in Christian circles we busy ourselves with "the ministry," very often operating out of a place of need rather than out of a response to the grace that God has given us.

When our motivation is anything outside of the love of God, the foundations on which we build our lives become cracked, and eventually they will fail. Our ministries struggle, our families suffer, and our relationship with God lacks the intimacy that He desires to have with us.

This book is about taking hold of the deepest love you'll ever experience and never letting go. Jack leads you to a place of being rooted and established in the Father's love where you are safe, secure and a success in all your relationships, especially with Him.

Jack was someone who said everything right, did everything right and from the outside looked like the perfect example of a born-again, Spirit-filled man of integrity running hard after God's kingdom. Everything would have suggested that he had it all together, and yet, in his heart there was a deep pain that no amount of performing, no amount of striving and no amount of covering could hide. He was desperately failing, and his family was falling apart.

In the midst of the pain and failure, God surprised Jack and embraced his life in a very special way. The Father revealed a measure of the depth of His love for Jack that completely changed the way he functioned in his ministry and in his family. This once hard-nosed, distant sea captain became a warm, tenderhearted father of both his family and ministry. One encounter with the Father's love revealed to Jack that he was loved not for what he could do but simply for who he is in Christ.

This revelation has radically transformed his family, his marriage and his ministry. God has now released Jack with this message, which he takes to the nations of the world. He is a regular guest speaker here in Toronto and often ministers at our School of Ministry. We love the powerful work of grace that God has done in Jack's heart, and we love how God uses Jack to minister deep levels of the Father's love in the lives of Christians everywhere.

I highly recommend this book for all Christians who minister to others or who simply want to go deeper with God. In all my years of being a Christian I have seen no other message expand peoples' hearts and enable them to grow with God in such great leaps and bounds. And I can think of no one whom I would more highly recommend to deliver this message than Jack Frost. His personal experience and testimony have opened a way into the Father's arms for anyone to follow. I know that this book will lead you deep into the Father's presence where you can receive the very thing you've been crying out for your entire life, *Experiencing the Father's Embrace*.

—JOHN G. ARNOTT

SENIOR PASTOR, TORONTO AIRPORT CHRISTIAN FELLOWSHIP

AUTHOR OF *THE FATHER'S BLESSING*

A REVELATION OF THE FATHER'S LOVE

Behold, I am going to send you Elijah the prophet before the coming of the great and terrible day of the Lord. And he will restore the hearts of the fathers to their children, and the hearts of the children to their fathers, lest I come and smite the land with a curse.

—MALACHI 4:5–6

Then comes the end, when He delivers up the kingdom to the God and Father, when He has abolished all rule and all authority and power.

—1 CORINTHIANS 15:24

We are living in possibly the greatest moment since the beginning of time, when God has begun to restore all things to His sons and daughters in order to prepare them for a great End-Time revival. These verses imply that all things began with the Father, and in the end, all things will end with a deeper revelation of the Father.

In the January 1990 issue of *Charisma* magazine, Paul Cain, a prophetic voice to the world, was asked: "What do you believe the decade of the 1990s holds for the church?" His answer: "I believe the church is about to experience a revelation of the Fatherhood of God. A new wave of evangelism will result as millions of prodigals will see the Father's love in the church again."

In the late 1980s, much of the church had grown lukewarm or complacent in their love for God. Much of it was because we sought to consume the blessings of God upon our own lusts for position, power or possessions. We continued in our duty, as the voice of the Lord grew dim. We applied our energies to ministry and religious activity. There was a lack of experiential understanding of the Father's love for His children; thus, many sought for various levels of His love and intimacy through works. In the early part of the 1990s, Father began drawing us back home to Him by releasing renewal upon the church once more.

Now, at the turn of the century, the Father has begun to prepare His church to become the Father's house so that millions of prodigals and the lost will see the Father's love, compassion and forgiveness in us, and thus will desire to come home to the Father. We no longer are just learning about the Father's love; many are experiencing the Holy Spirit breaking forth the Father's love in their area of need: "The love of God has been poured out within our hearts…" (Rom. 5:5). It is no longer enough to just teach on the Father's love. We are living in an hour when we must begin to minister out of a deep personal experience we have had in the Father's affectionate love.

Chapter One

My Encounter
With the Father's
Embrace

I couldn't believe what I was hearing. It was the voice of my stern, disapproving father saying the words I had longed to hear for so many years.

"Son, I love you. Everything is going to be all right."

It was 1972. Because of an LSD overdose, I lay in a semicomatose state in a hospital bed in Daytona Beach, Florida. My dad was cradling me in his arms and running his fingers through my shoulder-length hair, telling me—his rebellious, misfit son—that he really loved me.

This couldn't be happening, I thought to myself as I listened to the faint beeping of medical equipment. My dad was telling me he loved me! This was the same overpowering dad who months earlier had shoved me to the floor in our home, grabbed a pair of scissors and violently cut off my hippie-style hair after telling me I was a disgrace to the family. Now he was tenderly whispering to me about love, forgiveness and acceptance. Even though I was in a drug-induced fog, his words sank deep into my soul.

"Son, I love you."

As a boy, I had longed for Dad's approval and affection. I just wanted him to smile at me or to say that he was proud to be my dad. Yet when I opened my heart to receive his love, I always was left empty and disappointed. I was now nineteen years old, yet I could not remember one time in my life when my dad had held me close or said those words. As a result of the rejection I felt, I had ceased being my father's son and never wanted to see him again.

Like so many men from his generation, Dad didn't know how

to express affection. He was a good man and would have died for me. But to him, showing emotion was a sign of weakness. Because he had grown up during the Great Depression and lived in a fatherless home, he built a fortress around his heart to protect himself from pain. Then he went to war and learned even more survival skills. Later, he expressed his love simply by providing for his family financially and by teaching his two sons to survive in a merciless world. He always told me, "Never be weak by showing emotions or tears! Be tough! Be a man!"

For years I had tried unsuccessfully to be the tough man that my father wanted me to be. Yet as I lay in that hospital bed at a time of ultimate failure, Dad was holding me in his arms and expressing love for me. He was not aware that I could hear his voice or that I could feel his arms around me. I had been willing to stop being my father's son, but my father was not willing to stop being my father. His commitment to me was greater than my commitment to him.

That was perhaps my first glimpse of Father God's unconditional love—and of His desire to express His affection to me, even though I had failed miserably. It would be several more years before I would take the first step to receive that amazing love.

DRIVEN TO ACHIEVE

Dad was a respected man in our community, and his athletic abilities—particularly his skills as a professional tennis instructor—won him plenty of honors in Daytona Beach. I tried to meet my dad's expectations in sports and to perform well enough to earn his approval, but I was awkward with a tennis racquet and never seemed to impress him. Dad regularly reminded me—in harsh words—that I wasn't good enough.

He would scream at me like a drill sergeant when we practiced on Saturday mornings: "Put your arm into it! Be a monster! Don't be such a wimp!"

These ordeals would leave me in tears. I felt like such a failure, yet I wanted Dad's approval so much I kept striving to perform for him. *If only I could hit the ball right,* I told myself, *then Dad will be proud of me.* I did not realize that an ungodly belief was growing stronger and stronger in me. I was slowly being consumed by a deep fear of failure and rejection, a fear that caused me to feel worthless unless I performed well enough to win my father's approval.

This ungodly belief produced unhealthy results in my twenties when I became a commercial snapper and grouper fishing boat captain. Driven by a relentless desire to prove myself, I aspired to become the best fisherman on the southeastern coast of the United States. Everything I did in life began to revolve around my dream to become what people in the fishing business call "top hook."

Like my father, I had to be the toughest and the best. And like my father, I developed a fierce temper. Any member of my crew who caused us to lose fish or who disappointed me in any way faced the brunt of my anger. I became known as the Captain Bligh of the Carolina coast. I was a screamer and a tyrant. People did not want to mess with Jack Frost in those days.

I would often risk the lives of the crew by spending a week or more off the Carolina coast in the winter, riding out forty- to sixty-miles-per-hour gales and twenty- to thirty-foot seas in a forty-four-foot boat so we could claim the coveted prize—"top hook." I was driven by my fear of failure and by a cruel ambition that left no room for compassion for anyone. I had to be the winner at all costs. In my warped way of thinking, I was nobody if I did not outfish everybody. I did not realize that deep inside, I was consumed by an unconscious desire to win my father's approval. That nagging void had become a cancer that was eating me alive.

But everything changed in 1980. That's when God's overwhelming love finally broke through. I was twenty-seven years old at the time, and my life was in shambles. I had been addicted to drugs, alcohol and pornography for more than ten years because I was constantly seeking a way to escape the pain caused by the fear of failure. My anger was out of control, and as a result, I constantly wounded my wife, my son and others with my words and demeaning looks.

In a desperate attempt to escape this pain, I took my fishing boat out to sea one day in February 1980. Once I got forty miles off the North Carolina coast, I cried out to God for three days, asking Him to make Himself real to me.

"O God," I said, "please do something. I've hurt everyone around me. I'm miserable. I don't know why I feel so driven. It's like something inside me is pushing me to the edge of insanity. I don't know why I am so harsh. I feel like I am being poisoned from the inside. Please help me."

It was then, when I was at the lowest place in my life, that I encountered the unconditional love of Christ for the first time. Instantly His presence broke the chains of alcoholism, drug addiction and pornography. In a moment's time God gave me a new heart. The burden of sin lifted, and I felt true joy for the first time.

I had tasted of the Lord's goodness. But it would take years for me to find total deliverance from the fear of failure and the aggressive striving that had made me such a driven man.

PERFORMING FOR GOD

After my conversion, I became active in church life and quickly learned that my tendency toward performance operated well in a religious environment. I simply transferred my ungodly beliefs, my fear of failure and my aggressive striving into church work. I thought that the best way to win God's approval and acceptance was to do things for Him and also to win the favor of the Christians around me.

It seemed to be perfectly natural to express my love for God by building my identity through hyperreligious activity. Many of the Christians around me seemed to think the same way. The more we prayed, fasted, read our Bibles, witnessed to strangers or attended church meetings, the more acceptance we thought we gained from God.

But this false understanding of God's character came with a high price. After working so hard to please Him, I had no lasting joy, no peace, no rest and no energy left to convince my wife and children that I loved them more than ministry.

As I began to pastor a small church in 1984, my childhood filter system for earning love and acceptance translated ministry into an aggressive zeal to win souls and build the fastest-growing church in our denominational district. Just as I had been willing to do anything to be the best fisherman in the southeastern United States, now—as a Christian leader—I wanted to achieve my spiritual goals so I would receive the praises of men. Unconsciously, I was driven by a need to be needed.

I wanted to look good to everybody. But underneath the veneer of success, I was an unhappy man with a miserable family. My commitment to "the ministry" was far greater than my commitment to my wife, my children or any other loving relationships. When I was at home, I was irritable and impossible to get along with. Everything I did was tainted with a passive anger.

My countenance became stern and serious, and my preaching became legalistic and demanding. I focused on biblical truth, but my heart was empty of love. I knew the theology of God's love, but I had not experienced it in my relationships. I could quote verses in Scripture about His unconditional acceptance of us, but it was a foreign concept to me.

As a result, I began comparing myself to others in ministry, thinking they were more blessed or more gifted than I was. This fostered a competitive attitude, rooted in jealousy, that made it almost impossible for me to relate to other ministers or to anyone in spiritual authority in a healthy way. I became a master of disguises. I would sit at ministers' conferences with a smile on my face. But underneath my clever religious mask, I viewed successful church leaders with an attitude of rivalry and judgmentalism.

I couldn't stand the thought that they might be successful. If they were blessed, I felt deprived. If they experienced some form of failure, I secretly rejoiced. My heart was sick with pride.

Finally in 1986 I acknowledged my need for healing and went through some deep, healing prayer ministry to uncover the roots of anger, drivenness and lack of intimacy. This experience impacted so many areas of my life that by 1988, my wife, Trisha, and I spent the next seven years teaching seminars about emotional healing in many churches throughout the country.

I thought I was free! Trisha and I were effective in ministering to pastors and other church leaders as we helped them find healing in their marriages and families. But I soon realized that my own deep struggle with performance orientation was not resolved. Even after we began the healing prayer ministry, I would often fall back into my old habit patterns of aggressive striving. I kept giving my wife those demeaning looks and speaking to her in stern and rigid tones. And when I was caught in this cycle, I couldn't see that I was the one at fault.

Outwardly, I was a man of moral integrity and godly character as a Christian. I never had a moral failure. I was an aggressive pursuer of God, praying and reading the Bible for two or three hours a day and doing all the right religious things. But inwardly I lacked the ability to express love at home. I was joyless. I had no inner peace. I was driven by spiritual ambition because I had built my identity and value systems on position, power and possessions. My faithfulness, duty and service were not a response of true love to God; they flowed instead from a desire for personal gain and reward.

I could not see the bondage I was in, but my family could! I felt I gave my wife nothing to complain about. After all, I was faithful to her and always provided for her needs. Trisha knew I would be home every night and remain loyal to her. I was a man committed to purity in marriage. I had not touched pornography since my first encounter with Jesus. I even told her every day that I loved her.

But there was a lack of warmth and tenderness, and she felt unloved and rejected. Daily she battled the pain of being married to a man who gave his life to meet everyone else's needs (and his own), but who did not have energy left to make his wife believe she was loved more than the ministry. As a result she had to wear her own disguises, suppressing the guilt and anger she constantly felt because her need for intimacy and emotional bonding wasn't being met. She fell into a severe depression, and well-intentioned church people made her feel guiltier.

"You are married to such a godly man," they would tell her. "You should be grateful instead of having these negative thoughts about him." After twenty years of living like this, Trisha was dying inside. Any hope for a better marriage was gone.

My children didn't fare any better. As more legalism crept into my life, the more unyielding and joyless I became as a parent. My three children could never do things well enough for me. They didn't make good enough grades, they didn't perform well enough in sports, and they never did their household chores to my satisfaction.

I would tell them I loved them, but I constantly pointed out every mistake and shortcoming. I demanded exact obedience, but I lacked the ability to express love, tender affection and grace and mercy when they fell short. I read all the proper parenting books and tried measuring up to every expert's standards, but something seemed to hinder me from expressing the love I felt inside.

By 1995, my seventeen-year-old son and my fourteen-year-old daughter had closed their spirits to any affection, correction or advice I tried to offer them. They stopped looking me in the eye because they feared the look of rejection I often gave. They hardly spoke to me because they were afraid of upsetting or displeasing me. My pride produced a desire in them to rebel, and they began to seek the acceptance they yearned for by hanging around the wrong crowd. And worst of all, they wanted nothing to do with the angry, legalistic God I modeled to them.

TEARS OF HEALING

Even though my family life was in shambles, God was still at work. In 1994, while I was attending a spiritual renewal conference, He began bringing me a fresh revelation of His power and grace. There were times that I spent hours weeping at the altar. Yet during these dramatic encounters, I never equated His presence with what I know now as God's *phileo* love.

Phileo is a Greek word that means "demonstrated, natural affection." (See John 16:27.) It is occasionally used in the Bible to describe God's love. Yet I always tended to view God's anointing as His *power*—or His supernatural ability to do great things. I had no idea that His anointing could actually be a demonstration of His unconditional affection for me. I was so locked into this trap of performance orientation that I still did not break free from my aggressive striving—even after a powerful visitation of God's Spirit! In fact, as I experienced more favor and visibility in ministry, my addiction to striving grew even stronger!

At that point my family had experienced enough of what I wrongly called "ministry." My wife and children knew I was worshiping a golden calf of self-centered religious pride. The ministry was all I talked about, all I lived for and all that brought a smile to my face. I felt inadequate at expressing love and care for my family, so I gave myself to what I could do well—the ministry. It made everyone at home miserable. Trisha had had more than she could take. I was doing all the right, religious things, yet our family was teetering on the edge of disaster.

Thinking that it was Trisha who had the real problem, I took her to a conference on emotional healing in November 1995. I wanted her to be happy with how God was using me in ministry so she would finally develop an appreciation for all the sacrifices I had made for her.

During an afternoon pastors' session, many of the wives were at the front receiving prayer. Trisha was resting on the floor, praying and weeping quietly as I knelt beside her. Then someone from the platform began to pray. The words startled me:

> *"Father God, take all the men in this room who were never held by their fathers. Hold them close right now. Give them the love their fathers did not know how to give."*

The anointing of the Holy Spirit fell on me immediately. I did not understand what was happening, but it felt as if hot, liquid love was pouring into my soul. I began crying like a baby as I lay at the altar. Such displays of emotion were not normal for me. I always had every emotion in check, especially in front of my wife, children or other ministers. But my mask was off now. I was completely undone.

It was as if God transported me back to a time when I was only ten. I suddenly saw vivid scenes of me as a child, hiding in a closet at night, fearful of the yelling and screaming I heard in my parents' room. I remembered the fear, the loneliness and the sense of abandonment. I felt the deep, painful ache for my father's embrace—an embrace he was not able to give me during my childhood.

Suddenly I realized that now, thirty-four years later, my heavenly Father was meeting the deepest need in my heart for a natural demonstration of a father's affectionate love. I had a direct encounter with the *phileo* of God. As I lay on the floor weeping, Father God entered that dark closet of my childhood and held me in His arms. For forty-five minutes, the Holy Spirit poured the love of God that the apostle Paul spoke of in Romans 5:5 through my body and washed away much of the guilt, shame, fear of failure and rejection, fear of intimacy and the fear of receiving and giving love.

My breakthrough finally came. My pride had been shattered. Until that moment I had never realized how deeply in bondage I was to striving and fear. You do not know what you are in bondage to until you are free from it! But in that instant I felt free, and for the first time I experienced true rest. I had heard all my life that God loved me, but I had never lowered the walls of protection enough to receive personally a natural demonstration of His love and affection in some of my deepest areas of core pain. Knowledge of His love had become a personal experience! *Phileo* was no longer just a Greek word to use to construct a theology.

I didn't stop weeping for five months. Every time I looked into my wife's eyes or saw the pain that I had caused my children because of my lack of tenderness, the tears would begin to flow. Then I would kneel at their feet, weeping and pleading for forgiveness for the times I had harshly misrepresented the Father's love to them.

I knew the healing would not come instantly for them. My children's hearts had been closed to me for years. But now, the brokenness I was experiencing began to open their spirits. The Father's affectionate *phileo* love began to restore the heart of this father to his children and the hearts of my children to their father, and it was breaking a curse off of our lives. (See Malachi 4:6.)

Four months after I received this unusual baptism of the Father's love, my daughter, Sarah, gave me an essay she had written for her English class at school. It was titled "The Greatest Influence in My Life Is..." My eyes moistened as I began to read her words:

> The greatest influence in my life is my daddy! Through him, I have seen the eyes of Jesus and felt His unending love! At one point, not very long ago, my daddy was a man to fear. He was Captain Bligh off the *H.M.S. Bounty*. Now he is as gentle as a lamb, not to mention just as loving. Through watching my daddy change from being a hard man to being

tender, he has influenced me to change. His new patience has helped bring me through a very difficult year. Seeing my father love and cherish God, like never before, has done miracles for me. Instead of referring to God like a Holy Being, he refers to Him as Daddy.

Now, instead of fearing my dad, I crawl up in his lap, and I find a very cherished peace. What I cherish most about my father is his smile. I also love the way he sits with me and helps me with my faults in a loving way. Whenever I do something good, he notices that, too. My dad is changing in so many areas. I am so proud of him. Every time he looks at me and smiles, I explode inside with joy. My daddy has been my greatest influence these past four months. I forgive him for being Captain Bligh in my early years. I love you, Daddy!

This overpowering revelation of the Father's love also began transforming my marriage, but it didn't happen overnight.

I had rarely been able to pray with or minister to my wife prior to my encounter in 1995. In spite of the breakthroughs I experienced with my children, something in me seemed to hold back from pursuing deeper levels of intimacy with Trisha. Because of some traumatic experiences of my childhood, I always kept my emotions and feelings under control around her. I daily said the words "I love you," but I could not let Trisha inside. I did not want to risk being hurt again.

In March 1996 I went with a group of men to a conference in Canada, seeking a deeper revelation of God's love. During the first meeting, a lady at the altar prayed with me about some deep hurts I had encountered as a young boy. Through the supernatural leading of the Holy Spirit, this woman discerned that around age ten I had constructed thick walls of protection in my soul during the time that my father and mother were having extreme difficulties in their marriage.

This woman's prayers laid my heart bare. I lay on the floor weeping uncontrollably for two hours as the Father poured His comfort, love and affection into my wounded heart. When I got up, I knew that the wounds I experienced so long ago had been healed.

Then, during a subsequent ministry time that evening, what seemed like a river of God's love broke through all my fears of intimacy, and the walls I built so long ago began to crumble. For the next four days I wept as I realized the depth of pain Trisha lived with daily. She had always been kept at arm's length from the heart of her husband. I had unconsciously pushed her away. But when I arrived home from that conference I intimately ministered my love to her in healing prayer. She wept for hours as the Father took her back to some points of deep wounding in her youth, comforting her with His healing love.

God began to take our relationship into new depths of intimacy. We have hit a few stumbling blocks along the way, but each time the Holy Spirit would reveal past hurts where we had built walls of protection. We would move toward repentance, and the love of God would wash away hidden barriers and take us into deeper depths of love for each other.

During one of these times in 1998, I was prompted to write my wife a poem. I am not a poetic type, and writing these kinds of words was extremely uncharacteristic of me. But it evidences the power of the Father's love to transform the most callous husband!

SUCH A LOVE

Our journey has taken us throughout the earth
From pain and suffering our love did birth
Yet love did flourish from the shame and tears
Our love remained true all through the years!

What pain can hold back such a love as ours
Not shame, not fear, not even wounded hearts
For our love has conquered every wall
It has fought and grasped for passion's call!

It was your love that brought to me a rest
A love that my pain has put to the test
Yet you endured and gave of your best
Today it is the reason I feel so blessed!

What kind of woman could love as you do?
One who is beautiful, faithful and true.
It takes one whose heart is made of pure gold
One whose life will be as a tale that is told!

Your love will be spoken of for ages to come
For it is the kind that lights up the sun
It is full of fire, passion and zeal
A love that is not false but open and heals!

Your love fills my heart with visions and dreams
Faith, hope and love my heart has finally seen
Your love has given me reason to live
Your love has caused my heart to want to give!

How could your love be so rich and free?
How could you love such a man as me?
How could your heart be filled with such desire?
How could you cause me to burn with such fire?

Certainly your love must come from above
How else could you know such a wondrous love
I long to return that love to you one day
With such desire and self-sacrifice may I love, I pray!

O God, I could never repay what You have done for me
When You gave me her love, so beautiful, so free
Forgive me for all the years that I did blame
As an excuse not to love, because of my pain!

Unmerited favor I received when I first saw her face
Your love, through her, has revealed to me grace
Now I am honored to call her my wife

I will cherish and care for her all of my life!

I would go through the pain again and again
To experience her love that covered my shame
I would give my life, my wealth and my fame
To love her and cherish her and give her my name!

When I finished reading this poem to Trisha, she began to weep with deep, convulsing sobs. It was as if the excruciating pain she had hidden inside for so long began to pour out of her. After about ten minutes the sobbing turned to gentle tears of peace and joy.

"All of these years I never really could believe you loved me," Trisha told me. "For the first time, I now know it is true. I now feel loved by you!"

As the Father's love has brought restoration of intimacy to my marriage and family, it has changed my whole philosophy of ministry as well. I am no longer striving to be holy or to win God's favor. I don't want to do anything to hinder the intimate, loving relationships that God has given me. Ministry is no longer something that I have to work or strive for. The comparisons, competition and rivalry are fading away. Spiritual ambition is now but a shadow.

Most of the time I am motivated by a deep gratitude for being loved and accepted unconditionally by my Father. Ministry is simply an overflow of the love of God that flows freely through my marriage and family. As I receive His natural demonstration of affection for me, His precious *phileo* love, then I simply give it away to the next person I meet.

This restoration of love and intimacy in my life has been a process that has required deepening levels of humility and repentance on my part. I have certainly not arrived! I can easily get off center of the Father's love when my priorities get confused. I can still be pulled toward aggressive striving. But now, I do not stay in that condition for long. I quickly run back into the resting place of the Father's healing love, and peace is restored to my heart. I am then compelled to humble myself and repent to anyone who has been hurt by my striving. And I am then restored once more to a life of intimacy and love!

Do you know what it means to love God wholeheartedly? Is love for God reflected in faithful Bible reading, rigorous prayer or strict holiness? I think not. What reveals a genuine love for God is my ability to convince my family and others of my love for them. Without this, everything else finds its rewards in self-love. Doing great things—even religious things like preaching, winning souls, performing miracles or feeding the poor—all have their own rewards. And we can do these things out of wrong motives. But the Bible tells us that we cannot say we love God if we do not love each other (1 John 4:20).

Do you desire to know fully the Father's love for you? Would you like to encounter His unconditional affection? This book contains many of the precious truths that I have experienced and learned about the Father's love since I was touched so deeply in 1995. As you read and study these pages, I pray that you will do much more than develop a healthy theology. Rather, I pray you will experience your Father's affectionate embrace, feel His unconditional acceptance and hear His tender words of love in deeper ways than you have ever known.

I pray you will hear the words that the Father spoke to His beloved Son in Mark 1:11: "Child, you are the one I love, and on you My favor rests" (author's paraphrase).

QUESTIONS FOR DISCUSSION

1. Describe your relationship with your own father and mother. Did you always feel unconditionally loved by them? If not, do you think this has affected the way you view your heavenly Father? In what ways?

2. Many people struggle to believe that God loves them unconditionally. They may feel ashamed of something from the past, or they may think that they must perform certain duties in order to win God's approval. In your life, what is the biggest hindrance to believing that God really loves you?

3. Think about the relationships in your life. Do the people who are closest to you see the love of God in your life? If not, what do you need to experience in order to reflect God's love to them?

Chapter Two

You Were Created
for Love

After Nicolae Ceausescu's dictatorship ended in Romania in 1989, the world was horrified to learn that thousands of Romanian children had been forced to live in poorly managed state-run orphanages. Because Ceausescu had outlawed all forms of birth control, poor parents often turned their newborns over to the authorities or simply abandoned them in the streets. The youngsters were unwanted at birth and completely neglected when they arrived at these crude institutions.

Often starving, babies were locked in their cribs like caged animals. Toddlers were chained to their highchairs for hours. Workers ignored the children's cries and rarely changed their diapers. These hellish facilities—resembling child-sized versions of Nazi prison camps—existed for more than a decade in Romania. But when communism collapsed in Eastern Europe, human rights organizations learned just how cruel Ceausescu's regime had been to the most vulnerable of its citizens.

Many Westerners rushed into the country to adopt these love-starved children after seeing televised news reports of the atrocities in Romania. But in the mid-1990s, the adoptive parents learned firsthand what psychologists had already predicted. These children, who had never known the love of a father or mother, and who had never been held, consoled or shown any form of affection, had been mentally and emotionally crippled beyond repair. They had developed what professional counselors call *reactive attachment disorder.*

Children with this condition cannot function normally. At an early age ungodly beliefs begin to influence their personality.

They begin to believe that adults are uncaring, abusive and unreliable. Because they were neglected for so long, they lose the ability to trust. Because they were not nursed or fed properly, normal childhood development goes haywire. Because they have never been hugged, they cannot give love, but they live for self-love, seeking to get their unhealed needs met. In order to escape the pain of rejection, they become self-destructive. They also develop uncontrollable anger, severe hyperactivity, learning disorders and compulsive tendencies such as lying, stealing or hoarding food.

Sadly, many of these children are still struggling with incredible psychological trauma because of the way they were abused or neglected as youngsters. Others were not even that fortunate. They did not live to see their twelfth birthdays.

They died simply from a lack of love!

It is no secret that human beings need affection to thrive. Scientists have actually proven that humans are four to seven times more likely to succumb to sickness if they do not have a normal dose of nurturing love. Some studies have shown that people recover from illness quicker if they have a human being— or even a pet—to supply that tenderness.

Caring words, friendship, affectionate touch—all of these have a healing quality. Why? *Because we were all created by God to give and receive love.* If we do not receive it and learn to give it away, we will suffer emotionally and never reach our God-given potential.

I understand this today, but there was a time in my life when I thought I could live without love. Because of the level of rejection that I experienced as a child, I shut people out of my life at an early age. I decided I could live my life in isolation, without anyone else's help. People were a source of pain, so I decided to keep them at a distance.

My father was the same way. He was part of the self-made World War II generation. He knew what it meant to claw and scrape through economic hardship without anyone else's help. He was a survivor. He had closed his heart to love so that he couldn't feel the pain that throbbed inside his soul. And he passed that pain on to me like some kind of inherited disease. Harshness and isolation were part of my spiritual DNA.

By the time I was twelve years old I had decided that I didn't need anybody. By age twenty-four I was captain of my own fishing boat. I was strong, self-confident and detached. I relished the fact that I could do it alone. I learned to be successful, to provide for my family and to build my reputation.

I loved it when people said to me, "Man, how did you do that? How did you survive that storm? How did you stay out on the ocean for so many days?" I didn't need intimacy with another person. It was just me and the sea. Because I couldn't bond in healthy relationships, I bonded to the ocean and to my career as a commercial snapper fisherman. Then when I came to Christ and still didn't know how to bond in healthy relationships, I began searching for another counterfeit affection. I found it in the ministry.

There is nothing easier than self-deception. *I thought love was about what we do.* I thought that if I could really impress people and become a success in the worldly sense, I could win the affirmation I craved. I didn't know that love is not about what we do, but who we are, convincing others of our love for them…and about who loves us.

FOUR KEYS TO INTIMACY

Love should come naturally to us. We were created by God to love and to be loved. But because we were born into a sinful world, and because our sinful nature was bent toward believing the worst about God—rather than choosing to know Him as the loving Father that He is—we find that accepting His love and giving it away to others is a struggle even after we initially come to accept Christ's salvation. Our minds need to be renewed by the Holy Spirit until we truly can say as the apostle John declared,

"And we *have come to know [experience] and have believed* the love which God has for us. God is love" (1 John 4:16, emphasis added).

That verse goes on to say, "God is love, and the one who *abides in love* abides in God, and God abides in him" (emphasis added). Notice that it does not say that God abides with the person who preaches eloquently or who attends church every week or who fasts fifty days every year. It does not say that God abides with the person who prays faithfully every day or who knows how to cast out demons or win souls to Christ. It says that God abides with the person who is at home with love.

Are you comfortable with love? Are you continually filled with the understanding of how much the Father loves you? Are you aware that the Father takes delight in you and that He thinks about you all the time? (See Psalm 139:17–18.) Do you realize that He feels nothing but perfect love when He thinks about you? First Corinthians 13:5 tells us that "love thinks no evil" (NKJV).

Most of us struggle through life because we are afraid to receive and give love. We are basically afraid of intimacy (*in-to-me-see*). Either because of a deficiency of parental love or because we experienced some traumatic form of rejection in the past, we set up boundaries and walls to keep people out so that we can protect ourselves from the pain of more rejection. This hinders us from having intimate fellowship with God and healthy relationships with others.

At the core of this fear is *deception*. We find it difficult to love because we have believed a lie about God. The enemy, who is described as "the father of lies" in John 8:44, continually lies to us about the character of the Father. Our adversary tells us that God does not love us unless we perform well enough to earn His love. He tells us that God is abusive, angry, aloof, impatient and constantly disappointed with us. If the enemy of our souls can convince us that God has rejected us, is upset with us or has withdrawn from us because of some sin we committed, he knows we will hide from God and try to live our lives performing well enough to earn His love, thus increasing the depth of our guilt and shame.

I've identified four important keys to discovering genuine intimacy in relationships—both with our heavenly Father and with others. If we understand these principles, we can begin breaking through the lies and fears that prevent us from truly knowing and believing that God loves us unconditionally.

Key #1: The image you have of yourself will determine the level of intimacy in which you can walk.

You were created in God's image, and God is love. If you are uncomfortable with God, you are uncomfortable with love. If you are uncomfortable with love, you are uncomfortable with yourself. If you are uncomfortable with yourself, you're going to be uncomfortable with others. If you don't believe you are lovable, you find it difficult to receive God's gift of unmerited love and favor. And there is no way you can enjoy normal relationships with others if you view yourself differently from the way God views you.

In whose image do you walk? Your image of yourself will determine the depth of intimacy you will have with God, your spouse, your children and your friends. And if your self-image is based on how well you perform, you are headed for disaster. If you derive your self-worth from how well you do your job or from some kind of spiritual achievement or ministry success, then your self-image needs some change.

Do you see yourself as a lover created in God's image and a lover of other people? When you are away from your family, do you think about them, anxious for the moment when you can wrap your arms around him or her again? Are you able to share openly and honestly with your spouse about your deepest hurts and struggles? Are you free to shower praise and affection on your children? Are you able to encourage them—or do they only know of your correction, criticism and disapproval? Are you free to love those friends and family members around you?

Or have you bought into the lie that says you don't need to express love? Men in particular struggle with this ungodly belief. When I start talking about intimacy, tenderness and emotional vulnerability, many guys head for the door. They're simply not interested. Talking about deep emotional needs is not on their radar screen. Many men would prefer to live their lives inside a thick suit of armor—always pretending, always with their guard up, never sharing their true feelings. By the time they are old men, they are simply hollow shells. How tragic! They have become numb to love. They bought a lie that says men don't feel, men don't cry, men don't get in touch with their emotions. In essence, many men—and I'm talking here about Christian men who have surrendered their lives to Christ—do not really believe they are called to love. Some men even believe that it is not masculine to be tender and loving.

The problem with this ungodly belief is that it completely contradicts the essence of the gospel. The apostle Paul wrote words in 1 Corinthians 13 that are familiar to most of us:

> If I speak with the tongues of men and of angels, but do not have love, I have become a noisy gong or a clanging cymbal. And if I have the gift of prophecy, and know all mysteries and all knowledge; and if I have all faith, so as to remove mountains, but do not have love, I am nothing.
>
> —1 CORINTHIANS 13:1–2

What Paul is essentially saying is that the person who abides in love abides in God. Without love we have nothing because we are not abiding in God. Paul continues, "And if I give all my possessions to feed the poor, and if I deliver my body to be burned, but do not have love, it profits me nothing" (v. 3). Why would someone give all their possessions to feed the poor and yet not make such sacrifices from a motive of love? Why would they go to the mission field and die in some developing country and yet not demonstrate affection and love for their own family members? Why would a successful preacher give all of his time to the ministry and yet neglect or even abuse his wife and children?

These people would do these things because they are *trying to earn love and acceptance by their actions.* They are trying to earn God's approval because they don't truly understand His love. They have believed a lie, and it has warped their self-image.

A very successful guy once came to Jesus to find out how he could earn salvation. This man was a performance-oriented guy. He probably thought that he could buy Jesus' approval. So when he asked what he must do to be saved, Jesus said:

> "You shall love the Lord your God with all your heart, and with all your soul, and with all your mind." This is the great and foremost commandment. The second is like it, "You shall love your neighbor as yourself." On these two commandments depend the whole Law and the Prophets.
>
> —MATTHEW 22:37–40

Jesus said it's all about love. But we want to make this Christian life about everything else. We want it to be about rules or spiritual formulas or how we can impress God or win His favor. We have put the Great Commission before the *great commandment.* Born-again, Spirit-filled people who are eager to learn the latest spiritual truths and jump through the latest spiritual hoops never learned the Bible's most elementary lesson. In churches across this country, thousands upon thousands of Christians who grew up singing the kindergarten chorus "Jesus Loves Me, This I Know" have not experienced this truth to the deepest depths of their core need, receiving God's love and giving it away to the next person they meet.

Key #2: You must recognize your need for intimacy.
As much as you may think that you need to be independent

and self-sufficient, you were not created to live apart from God or others. Even Jesus Himself, who was the very image of God, was dependent on His Father. John 5:19 tells us that "the Son can do nothing of Himself, unless it is something He sees the Father doing." Through this humility and dependence, Christ has been given all dominion and authority.

Recently, my brother and I had the opportunity to really talk for the first time in thirty years. We were in the hospital with my father, discussing his impending death, and the conversation turned to the paths our lives had taken. My brother said to me, "You know, one thing I *can* say is that nobody has ever given me anything. Everything I've ever gotten has been because I've worked hard to get it." Thinking back over my own life, I responded, "Yeah, that's what happened to me, too." We were priding ourselves on our self-sufficiency and our independence, but we did not realize that that attitude is completely contrary to the nature God wants us to have. Both of us had struggled with intimacy and expressing love throughout our whole lives.

Have you bought into the idea that you should be able to pull yourself up by your own bootstraps and take care of yourself without help from anyone else? Would you rather close yourself off from other people than take a chance on really getting to know them? If so, it is a sin against love, believing that your self-sufficiency is all that you need. It may seem easier to focus on taking care of your own problems and surviving in a dog-eat-dog world, but in the long run you will have missed out on what is most important in life. God created us as human beings with the need for intimacy, to know and be known. And His perfect plan is to provide us with a beautiful way to meet that need: fellowship with Him and with each other. Why do we need to be intimate, loving beings so much? *Because we were created for love!* But before we can truly experience this love that God has for us, we must first recognize that our need for such love exists. We must realize that we cannot meet all of our needs on our own. We cannot control our emotions and destiny without it having generational impact for harm.

When God created Adam, He placed him in the Garden of Eden. God was so pleased with this creation that He called it "very good" (Gen. 1:31). Adam's needs were provided for: He had wonderful food to eat, a beautiful garden to enjoy and unhindered, intimate fellowship with his Creator. Adam walked with God every day, with no shadow of sin separating them.

Yet the Lord God knew all of this was not enough, saying, "It is not good for the man to be alone; I will make him a helper suitable for him" (Gen. 2:18). He then began to bring all the beasts of the field, the birds of the sky, every living creature, before Adam to see what he would call them. This was not just to give Adam something to do in his spare time. God had a purpose—to show Adam his need for intimacy.

Why do you suppose Eve was not created at the same time as Adam? Wasn't God smart enough to realize that man would be lonely? Didn't He know that He'd eventually have to create Eve? Of course God did. But He wanted Adam to have an understanding of his need. Before Eve was created, Adam's relationship with God became cemented, but that relationship with God wasn't all that his heart required—he had been created with the need for intimacy with a fellow human being. And because he began to understand that need, he was later able to truly love and cherish the woman God brought to him.

For many years, I kept my relationship with God separate from my wife. For seven years, I prayed two, sometimes three hours a day, with my wife shut out of my prayer closet. It was just God and me, together waiting for her to get her life straightened out. I believed I was the holy and righteous one because I was doing all the right, religious things, but all the while I was neglecting my relationship with my wife.

God wants us to have fellowship with Him, but a true relationship with God will not come at the expense of intimacy with our spouses and families. If you spend ten to eleven hours a day ministering to other people, but you spend very little time each day ministering to your spouse, your life is dangerously out of balance. I may have been focusing on a right relationship with God, but I had not recognized the deep need I had for true intimacy with my wife and family.

When Adam recognized his need for intimacy and love, God intervened on his behalf. The Lord God caused a deep sleep to come over Adam, and then He took one of Adam's ribs and lovingly fashioned for him a soul mate, a lover, a wife. Because Adam had first understood his need, he later knew when it had been fulfilled. And when he first laid eyes on his bride:

> And the man [Adam] said, "This is now bone of my bones, and flesh of my flesh; she shall be called Woman, because she was taken out of Man." For this cause a man shall leave his father and his mother, and shall cleave to his wife; and they shall become one flesh.
>
> —GENESIS 2:23–24

Adam and Eve stood before one another, naked and unashamed (*in-to-me-see*). Although they were two separate people, they became one flesh. They fully knew and were known by each other, with nothing hidden, nothing held back. What a beautiful picture of true intimacy!

Key #3: You must embrace your responsibility for intimacy.

Many relationship problems we have are a result of our unwillingness to know others and be known. This usually happens because we have been hurt or disappointed at some point in our lives, and we don't want to take that risk again. So we either deny our need for intimacy, or we place the blame on someone else—the person who hurt us.

Do you find yourself holding back in your relationships, unwilling to share your true self with your partner or mate? Have you been hurt in the past and find it difficult to trust? Are you afraid of further disappointment if you allow yourself to love again? Jesus came to restore our capacity for love and intimacy, despite all the many times we may have been hurt. Romans 8:16–17 tells us that "the Spirit Himself bears witness with our spirit that we are children of God, and if children, heirs also, heirs of God and fellow heirs with Christ." Through Christ, we inherit all the things that had been lost in the Fall—not only healing, joy and salvation, but also our capacity to love fully and to be loved.

By accepting Christ and becoming born again, you will receive all kinds of blessings, but if you don't have love and intimacy in your relationships, you have missed out on the fullness of what Jesus died for—to restore you to intimacy. If you flow in the gifts and do mighty exploits for the Lord, but you don't have love in your relationships with other people, all of your good works become null and void. It is your responsibility to choose to allow intimacy to become a priority in your life.

As Christians, what is the most important question we can ask of ourselves? How much of the Scripture have I studied? How many Bible conferences have I attended? How much faith do I have? All of these things are important, but they are not as important as the burning question: "Father, how can I receive Your love and give it to the next person I meet?" When I first began to ask myself that question, I tried to ask it daily. Then I learned that I needed to ask it hourly; now I understand that I must ask it of myself every ten or fifteen minutes. I can't wait to demonstrate the Father's love to everyone I meet, and especially to my wife and family, because this attitude must begin at home. If you are showing love to everyone else but denying true intimacy with your spouse, you are not accepting your full responsibility for walking in the Father's love.

In our modern Christian culture, the responsibility for intimacy has often fallen upon the female members of the household. The lie that men aren't supposed to feel or be tender and caring if they are to be considered masculine has pervaded even our church circles. Many Christian men shy away from the vulnerability that comes from sharing not only their emotions, but also their spiritual lives, with their wives and families. And when that happens, women often take up the slack.

Women tend to be the nurturers, the ones who are soft, caring and compassionate. They are usually the ones expected to "keep the home fires burning." Even our so-called biblical view seems to tell us that men should be the ones to provide, to go out and succeed in business and ministry. While the distinction between the roles of men and women is important, the Bible never says that a man cannot, or should not, be just as intimate and loving as a woman. Rather, Galatians 3:28 tells us that in Christ there is neither male nor female. God intends for men to experience tender intimacy, too.

When the Fall occurred in the Garden of Eden, both Adam and Eve sinned before God. But there was a difference between the two of them. Paul tells us in 2 Corinthians 11:3 that "the serpent deceived Eve by his craftiness," but in Romans 5:14, he tells us that Adam willfully sinned. Adam and Eve were both faced with the serpent; Eve fell under Satan's web of deception, but Adam sinned willfully. Then as they hid themselves from the presence of God, Adam was the one to whom God called, saying, "Where are you?" (Gen. 3:9). Although Eve had also sinned, Adam was the one God first held responsible. But when confronted with his sin, he turned the blame onto the woman, and at that point, the door for male irresponsibility in intimacy was opened wide.

Today many Christian men wear the fig leaf of fear: fear of rejection, fear of failure, fear of giving love, fear of receiving love, fear of intimacy. They hide in shame behind the fig leaves of their careers, or even their ministries, because they do not want to face the anxiety and insecurity they might experience if they were to be truly vulnerable with their wives. But God has called the man to protect his wife, to shield her and to love her as Christ loved the church. Christ sacrificed His very life for His bride; how many of us men are willing to sacrifice our self-love to meet the emotional needs of our wives? Both men and women must understand the importance of fostering intimacy in their lives and assume responsibility for taking the steps necessary to achieve it.

Key #4: Intimacy requires you to find your value and self-worth in who God created you to be.

So many of us base our self-worth on the things we do, what we can achieve, rather than who we are. This was a deception I struggled against for many years. I constantly asked myself, *How many people were set free under my ministry this week? How many testimonies came in from people who were touched by my teaching? How quickly is my ministry growing?* I began to live my life by the numbers. When I began to focus so strongly on what I had or had not achieved, I fell off center, away from the focus God wanted me to have. And that affected all of my relationships because it short-circuited my ability to be vulnerable with others.

Do you base your self-worth on how well your career is going? Do you need other people to praise your accomplishments in order to feel good about yourself? Let me ask the question another way. If you didn't get that promotion, or if you lost your job altogether, would you still feel good about yourself because you know in your heart that you are one of God's precious children? Would you live your life giving His love away to others? If you can't answer *yes* to those questions, you might be basing your self-worth on your own accomplishments rather than on who you are in Christ.

God's love, not your achievements, is what will fill the void in your life. When you truly grasp His deep and intimate love for you, it will fill you up to such an extent that the most natural thing in the world will be for you to share that love with everyone you meet.

Men, we are to love our wives as Christ loved the church (Eph.

5:25). Paul tells us that "husbands ought also to love their own wives as their own bodies" (v. 28). Before you can love your wife the way that God wants you to love her, you must first learn to love yourself. If you don't feel good about yourself, you won't be able to achieve true intimacy with your mate. The more we ask the Father to fill the void in our hearts and commit to practice loving actions to our spouses, children or others, the more comfortable we become with God and ultimately with ourselves. First John 4:16 says, "God is love, and the one who abides in love abides in God, and God abides in him." As we begin to submit to a lifestyle of love and intimacy, God is faithful to transform our heart, our character and our nature in ways we would never have imagined.

However, this submission requires a choice on our part. And sometimes we may not feel like making that choice. There are days when I come home in the evening, exhausted, and all my tired body wants to do is sit back in the recliner and watch a golf match on TV. But my wife will be in the kitchen, slaving over a hot stove to prepare my dinner, and I realize I need to make a choice to make love a priority. I go into the kitchen, put my arms around Trisha and tell her what a wonderful gift from God she is, that she is a treasure that can never be replaced. The rewards that come from making this choice are priceless. By practicing a lifestyle of love and intimacy, I open up my heart and allow the love of the Father to flow through me to my wife and my family.

I believe that the return of Christ is imminent. He is coming back soon, and the judgment day of His church is at hand. When I stand before that great, white throne to account for my life here on earth, I believe He will ask me just one question. It will not be, "In how many nations did you preach My Word?" It will not even be, "How many souls were saved, or how many people were healed under your ministry?" No, when I stand before the Lord to give an account of my life, I believe He will ask of me, "Jack, did you love your wife as I loved My church and gave Myself for her?" I hope that I will be able to answer *yes* on that day.

THE COMFORT OF FATHER GOD

All of the Law and the prophets' teaching in the Scriptures boil
down to the basic premise of love. God is love, and you were created for love, to experience intimacy with your heavenly Father
and with your fellow human beings. There should be nothing
more normal on earth than being a lover. In fact, it defies the law
of God's creation not to be comfortable with intimacy and love.

The four keys I have shared with you are important to help you
break through the deceptions about intimacy into which you
may have bought. They can help you begin to foster genuine intimacy in your relationships. But I have learned that you can't
withdraw from the bank what hasn't already been deposited
there. If you have never received genuine unconditional love in
your own life, it will be difficult for you to demonstrate that kind
of love to others. And if you have experienced not just a lack of
love, but any kind of abuse, it may be impossible for you to foster healthy relationships. Until you have an encounter with
Father God and allow His unconditional, affectionate love to fill
all the hurt and empty places in your heart, it may be difficult to
pour out love to others.

For the first twenty years of our marriage, my wife, Trisha, paid
the price because of hurts that I experienced in my childhood,
especially one traumatic incident involving my mother that
occurred when I was ten years old. God finally began to deal with
me in 1998 about these issues in my past that I thought had already
been resolved. Through prayer, counseling and deliverance, I had
forgiven my mother and broken the hurt and the pain associated
with that tragedy. But forgiveness and comfort are two very different things, and a little ten-year-old boy had been left uncomforted.
As a result, I took control of my own life and denied my need for
comfort. Because as a child I chose not to receive my mother's
expressed love, I was unable to pass tender, affectionate love on to
Trisha. Instead, the sea became my identity, and later the ministry,

leaving my wife to carry the wound of feeling I loved the sea and the ministry more than her.

In 1998, as I was being ministered to in a conference in Canada, God brought to my mind the memory of that ten-year-old boy and the deep trauma he had experienced. He gently showed me that even though I had received His deliverance in that event, there was still an ungodly belief there that was hindering my relationship with my wife. I needed a deep encounter with the love of Father God to fill up the void still in the heart of that ten-year-old boy. When I allowed His comfort to flow into those deep places of hurt, my heart began to open more freely to receiving nurture and comfort, and my relationship with my wife was able to reach deeper levels of intimacy.

Before we can have genuine relationships with others in which we allow ourselves to be honest, open and vulnerable, we must first experience the healing comfort of our heavenly Father in those areas of hurt and rejection in our hearts. You may have forgiven those people in your past who hurt you. You even may have experienced deliverance from inner vows you made as a result of those painful events. But have you allowed your Father God to wrap His loving arms around you and comfort you in those areas in which you have never felt comfort before?

God tells us that He has loved us with an everlasting love (Jer. 31:3). He longs to gather us to Himself as a mother hen gathers her chicks under her wings (Matt. 23:37). Don't allow the excuse of past hurts or abuse to cause you to miss out on the joy of deep, intimate communion in your relationships. Allow your Father to touch the deep places in your soul and to fill your heart so full of His love that it will spill out onto everyone around you.

You were created for love, for intimacy with God, with your spouse and with your family. God has crafted you to be an instrument of His love and to demonstrate His compassion and tenderness to everyone you meet. When you begin to experience His *phileo* love for you and allow it to flow through you to others, you will begin to experience true fulfillment because you will be doing what you were created to do.

If you want to experience this kind of intimacy and fulfillment in your life, begin by opening your heart to the Father and praying this prayer with me:

> *Father God, I believe that I have been created for love, to experience Your healing love and to share that love in my relationships with others. It's not enough to have success in my life or in my ministry if I don't have a relationship built upon expressed love with You or with my spouse and family. I renounce the lie that I am not a lover, that I cannot open up my emotions or allow myself to be hurt again. Instead, I ask You to wrap Your arms around me, to comfort me in those areas of hurt and pain and to fill me up so that I can in turn share Your love with those around me. I choose to love my family as Christ loved the church and gave Himself for her. I make a commitment to ask myself hourly, "Father, how can I receive Your love and then give it away to the next person I meet?" I want to live my life as an expression of Your love, no longer focusing on my own worldly successes but allowing Your character to shine through me. In Jesus' name, amen.*

QUESTIONS FOR DISCUSSION

1. Deceptions and ungodly beliefs that tell us we don't need love or that we are incapable of intimacy often prevent us from being genuine in our relationships. What kinds of lies or ungodly beliefs about intimacy have you bought into? How can God's love change your way of thinking in those areas?

2. Many people derive their self-esteem from the things that they do, their performance in their careers, their spiritual achievements or success in their ministries. What things cause you to feel good about yourself? Do you ever try to earn God's love and acceptance? If so, how can God's unconditional grace change this performance orientation?

3. In the Garden of Eden, Adam and Eve traded a perfect, unhindered intimacy with one another for the fig leaves of shame, vulnerability and fear. What fig leaves may be standing in the way of genuine intimacy with your mate and/or family? How can you humble yourself and allow God to restore communion in your relationship?

4. Are there any events in your past for which you may have received some healing and deliverance, but not the comfort of your loving heavenly Father? How can you humbly position yourself to begin to accept His comfort for those painful events in your life?

Chapter Three

You Are Father's Happy Thought

Y ou just wait till your father gets home!"
My wife had had it with our daughter. She had tried everything she knew to do, but nothing seemed to be working.
Sarah was sixteen years old and a typical teenager. Most of the
time, she was easy to live with, a true joy to her parents, but then
there were those days when no matter what went on, she would
be out of sorts. Around our house, that is called a "bad hair day."
It usually involves sulking, or pouting, or just a generally bad attitude. Unfortunately, when Sarah has a bad hair day, she can't just
keep it to herself. Everyone around her must join in her bad hair
day as well.

This particular episode was especially calamitous; for one thing,
Sarah's bad hair day had turned into a bad hair week, and to make
matters worse, Dad was out of town. Soon, as was to be expected,
Sarah's attitude became contagious, infecting her two brothers
who also just happened to be teenagers. My dear wife, Trisha,
patient as she is, was at her wit's end with three cranky adolescents
in the house and her husband out of town on a ministry trip.

Sure enough, the phone call came to my hotel room.

"Honey," my wife said, "I love you, and I love Sarah, but if you
don't hurry up and come home to deal with her, you may not
have a daughter when you finally *do* get here!"

When I asked her what had happened, she replied, "I'm so tired
of her negativity and mood spells. I honestly can't take living in
the same house with her anymore! I need you to come home and
take care of this."

I told Trisha that I could not cut my trip short and I didn't want to deal with it harshly over the phone. I knew my family needed my physical presence, but it would have to wait until I got home.

Trisha relayed the dreaded words to my daughter: "You just wait till your father gets home!" And Sarah knew that when I walked through the front door, the hammer was going to fall.

Although each member of my family understood that I loved them, they also knew my background of harshness and judgment. When I first accepted the Lord back in 1980, my life was transformed, and I was set free from drugs, alcohol and pornography—all at one time—never to return. But I easily fell into law and legalism. Becoming a legalistic holiness pastor, I preached hellfire and brimstone to my congregation. I preached more people out of heaven and into hell than I preached out of hell and into heaven. I valued obedience over relationship. Somehow I thought that if I could so easily turn my back on my former lifestyle, other people should be able to do the same. I had no tolerance for any perceived sin, whether it be an outright commission of wrongdoing or simply an attitude of the heart. I rained down guilt, shame and condemnation upon my congregation and my wife and children.

This was the dad that Sarah expected to meet when her father arrived home. And, boy, was she dreading the experience! But as I was driving back from my trip, the Holy Spirit began to prompt me to handle the situation in a different way, not with my usual lack of grace, but with the unconditional love of the Father. With that on my heart, I prayed the entire way home, "God, I really want to be a representation of Your love, not of the home environment I grew up in. I want to handle it the way You would handle it, demonstrating Your Father's comforting heart to Sarah."

When I arrived home, it was midmorning, and no one was home but my daughter. As I walked through the front door, she was waiting for me with a look of dread, failure and utter dejection on her face. She knew she had blown it, and she was almost cringing in anticipation of my disapproving, devaluing look.

This time, however, I didn't meet those expectations. I didn't come down on her immediately; I didn't even give her that "you-have-been-such-a-disappointment-to-your-father-again" look. Instead, I invited Sarah to go swimming with me at the public pool around the corner from our house. For an hour, we swam, we played, and we laughed, but all the while, Sarah was waiting for the hammer to fall.

By the time we returned to the house, the rest of the family was home. Laughter and play had caused Sarah to relax, and after we went inside, she headed for the bathroom to get cleaned up. As I went into the bedroom to begin unpacking my suitcase, I could hear her singing in the shower, "I've got the joy, joy, joy, joy down in my heart…And I'm so happy, so very happy…"

Trisha immediately looked at me and said, "Can you believe what a difference the presence of the father in the house makes?"

When you have failed and know you deserve the rod of judgment, what does the presence of the Father represent to you? What do you think when you hear the words, "You just wait till your father gets home!"? Do you picture God as the great policeman in the sky, waiting to pounce on any infraction of the law you may commit? Or is He your loving Daddy who brings the joy back to your heart, whom you can't wait to spend time with and who can't wait to spend time with you?

I did discipline Sarah later that day for her attitude and the way she had treated her mother and brothers. But I did it in tenderness and in love. When most Christians sin, they cringe, as Sarah did, expecting the full brunt of an angry God's wrath upon their heads. Most of us, when we have failed, picture the Father wagging His finger in our face in disapproval rather than envisioning His running toward us with arms open wide, eager to welcome us back into His presence. God certainly disciplines us, but it will never be in a way that imparts shame, fear or accusation. His motivation behind that discipline is His vast and eternal love for us. He does it for our good, for our betterment, because He wants the very best for us.

There is no fear in love; but perfect love casts out fear, because fear involves punishment.

—1 JOHN 4:18

THE RELIGION OF FEAR

Without a personal revelation of the Father's unconditional love, it becomes very easy to propagate the idea of a vengeful, angry God who can't wait to banish us to the fiery pit of hell. For many years, I believed in and vigorously preached that we sinners are only protected from the wrath of Father God by the compassionate nature of Jesus, who paid for our sins on the cross. Christ now intercedes for us, pleading with His Father to spare us the punishment we so rightly deserve. This almost schizophrenic view of the nature of God—that Jesus loves us but His stern Father is perpetually angry with us—has been ingrained in the mind-set of many Christians. While they can foster a deep and meaningful relationship with Jesus, they are at a loss when it comes to relating to intimacy with Father God.

If you walked into a church service and spotted someone who you knew was angry with you, you would probably head to the opposite side of the church to look for a seat. When there is a grudge being held or an ongoing disagreement, the people involved usually find a way to conveniently avoid one another, sometimes for years. Even in marriages, a husband and wife can live under the same roof, but if there is an undercurrent of anger or hostility in the relationship, a vast emotional distance will grow between them despite their close physical proximity.

It is impossible to have intimacy with someone who is mad at you. When we believe that God is angry with us, it is very difficult for us to accept His love or draw near to Him. When we do commit a sin, we say to ourselves, "Oh, what a holy God He is!" and, "Oh, what a wretched sinner I am!" Our image of God directly contrasts with the image we have of ourselves, and we run and hide as Adam did in the Garden of Eden.

Because we immediately dread God's wrath falling on our heads when we sin, we cannot freely run to Him for forgiveness; instead, we run to anything that seems safe and from which we can derive comfort. For some people, their addictions provide a safe and familiar environment, but running to these addictions can also cause them to spiral dangerously into a cycle of sin from which it is difficult to break free. For others, hyperreligious activity brings a sense of penance and gives false relief, thus offering a sense of comfort.

What pattern do you follow after you have fallen into sin? Are you afraid to come before God and freely confess your sin? Do you instead try to forget about what you have done, perhaps drowning your guilt in alcohol or some other addiction? Or do you do as I did, throwing yourself into a religious frenzy, trying to atone for your sin and appease an angry God with your good works and religious form and duty? If you follow any of these deadly cycles, you may be being influenced by a religion of fear and intimidation, and you need a new God for your old problems. You need a new image of God!

Religion has misrepresented the nature of Father God and portrayed Him to be something that He is not. The idea that the Father is the vengeful arm of the Trinity and Jesus the compassionate One, pleading for our undeserved pardon, is not just harmful to our relationship with God; it runs totally contrary to the teaching of Jesus.

Jesus came to demonstrate who the Father is and what He is like, and He does this through His words and His actions. To gain a true picture of the Father's feelings toward His children, it is best to turn to the One whose purpose it was to show us the Father. Jesus spent three years in ministry, demonstrating His Father's heart of compassion as He forgave sinners, healed the sick and raised the dead.

But even after all of that time, Philip, one of Jesus' closest followers, echoed a sentiment that many Christians today would like to say, "Show us the Father, and it is enough for us" (John 14:8).

Jesus' response is very telling: "Have I been so long with you, and yet you have not come to know Me, Philip? He who has seen Me has seen the Father…Do you not believe that I am in the Father, and the Father is in Me? The words that I say to you I do not speak on My own initiative, but the Father abiding in Me does His works" (vv. 9–10).

Jesus is the image of the invisible God and the exact representation of God's nature (Col. 1:15; Heb. 1:4).

The nature of the Father is the same as that of Jesus: He is love. And because God is love, everything He does, He does out of His love for us. We don't have to perform for Him or live a life of perfection in order to gain His approval. Even when we sin, the Father still loves us, and He longs to be the One to whom we run for comfort and forgiveness. God is love, and His perfect love casts out all fear (1 John 4:18). Everything Jesus did on earth, including His sacrificial death on the cross, shows us the heart of the Father, a heart of love and compassion, not one of wrath and judgment.

When we have an accurate understanding of the nature of our heavenly Father, we don't have an unhealthy fear of Him; we don't have to jump through hoops to please Him. The religion of fear will have no hold on us, and even when we sin, we can still crawl up into the lap of Father God and seek His love and forgiveness.

BEING AT HOME WITH GOD

At my house, we have a revolving front door; people from all over the world or even from right across town are constantly coming to visit. God has blessed us with a large and comfortable home that has room for plenty of guests to sleep, so we frequently house missionaries and pastors visiting from out of town. And with three children over the age of sixteen, our house has become the local hangout for many youth. There is rarely a dull moment with so much activity constantly taking place.

My wife and children love this arrangement; they can't wait for friends to arrive. I can't wait for friends to come, but I also can't wait for friends to leave. When there are visitors in the house, I can't always scratch where it itches. I can't just come home, let down my hair and relax; I have to be on my best behavior.

One good example of this involves my dietary habits. Twelve years ago, I became a vegetarian for medical reasons. Because I don't eat traditional forms of meat, I have to find alternative sources of protein for my diet, and one fantastic source of this is beans. I love to cook up a pot of fifteen-bean soup, letting it simmer on the stove for hours, and then eat off of it for several days, but such a nutritional regimen has its side effects. My sons love to have wars! Beans can truly be a magical fruit! For this reason, when there is company in the house and my wife sees me getting out the pot to cook up some fifteen-bean soup, she immediately tells me, "You are *not* going to cook that right now!"

Unless I know a visitor very well and feel comfortable enough around them to relax and be myself, I will not feel at home in my own house as long as they are there. Many Christians feel that way about God. Isaiah 66:1 tells us that God wants us to build a place for Him to live, a place in which He can relax and be with us and where we can relax and be with Him. But because we have so many misconceptions about our heavenly Father, we frequently don't truly feel at home in His presence if our house doesn't "smell" just right.

So often, well-meaning Christians pray for a *visitation* from God, but what He really wants is a *habitation* with us. He doesn't want to come into our lives as a guest while we are on our best behavior around Him until He leaves. He wants to be Someone around whom we can let our hair down and with whom we can share a pot of fifteen-bean soup. But if your image of the Father is of His pointing His finger of judgment in your face every time things don't "smell" right at home, you will never feel at home in His presence. You will be so busy striving to please Him that you won't be able to relax enough just to sit back with Him and enjoy the relationship. Martha made the same mistake, spending all of her time treating Jesus as a guest when what He really wanted her to do was relax and simply be with Him. Her sister, Mary, understood this and cherished her relationship, and as a result, Jesus said of her, "She has chosen the better way" (Luke 10:42, author's paraphrase).

I have known the Father both as a guest and as a true member of my household with whom I have intimate fellowship. For seven years, I spent at least three hours a day in my prayer closet and in the Word, but I never really knew who God was. I tried to be on my best behavior, hoping to gain His approval. Now I experience true intimacy with my heavenly Father because I understand that my relationship with Him is not based on what I do, but on what Jesus has done for me. Jesus was the man He was because of the Father He had. And I am the person I am because of the image of Father God I have. (See John 5:19; 8:38.)

Often, the result of the common misconception of the judgmental nature of the Father is our excessive striving to please Him, and when that ultimately fails, there is a feeling of shame and alienation from God's love. You cannot draw close to an angry God of whom you are afraid, and when you feel you must strive to gain His approval, you will begin to compete with other Christians around you. So many ministries are built, countries are evangelized and souls are won to the kingdom of God because Christians are trying to outdo one another for God's approval, to impress other people or to make them feel better about themselves. It's the story of so many Christians' lives. Lacking a true understanding of God's nature and character, they spend their lives aggressively striving for that elusive sense of love and acceptance, when all the while, the Father is reaching out to them, longing to have the intimacy and fellowship with them that Christ has already provided.

You Are Father's Happy Thought

Several years ago, the movie *Hook* was released, which told about Peter Pan's life after he grew up. He gradually lost his childlikeness and innocence until he finally reached a point when he had forgotten he was Peter Pan altogether. When the evil Captain Hook returned, kidnapped his son and daughter and whisked them off to Never-Never Land, Tinkerbell had to come to Peter Pan's assistance to help him remember who he was. In order to be able to fly and consequently be able to rescue his family from the clutches of Captain Hook, Peter Pan had to remember his happy thought.

When my daughter, Sarah, celebrated her sixteenth birthday, I happened to be out of town, and while I regretted missing the occasion, in a way it was fortunate for me. Sarah had never before been behind the wheel of a car, but she was about to experience that great rite of passage that all adolescents look forward to with great anticipation: the acquisition of her learner's permit. And due to my absence, the responsibility for Sarah's first driving lesson fell to my wife.

As can be found in many small towns, there is one street in our neighborhood that is notoriously dangerous; it has a sharp, hairpin curve with a swampy ditch that dropped off on both sides of the road. To make matters worse, it was only a short distance from the local high school, and each day when school let out, the teenagers would come flying down the street, taking the curve at fifty or sixty miles an hour.

Of course, this was the location chosen for my daughter's first driving lesson. And sure enough, just as she was approaching that hairpin turn, another teenage driver came barreling down the road straight toward her.

My wife, who has naturally red-tinted hair, began to "coach" Sarah rather vigorously about what to do in this situation.

"Get this car out of here! Can't you see what's about to happen? Watch out for that ditch!"

Sarah responded, "Would you just be quiet so I can think my happy thought?"

Even though my daughter had barely been behind the wheel for sixty seconds, she miraculously was able to avoid the ditches on both sides of the road and negotiate the car around the curve and into the church parking lot around the corner.

"That's it! This driving lesson is over. We will just have to wait until your father gets home for your next one!" my wife exclaimed in relief.

And then she thought to ask, "By the way, Sarah, what was your happy thought?"

Sarah replied, "Daddy. *Daddy would not be upset with me.* He would know what to do. That's what my happy thought was."

When you find yourself in a dangerous situation and fear grips your heart, what are the thoughts that bring you the most comfort and peace? When you experience the fear of failure or the fear of rejection, are your happy thoughts those of your heavenly Father, your Daddy who is not upset with you and who will know what to do? Or perhaps when you fall, your immediate thought is, *Oh, what a holy God He is and what a wretched sinner I am!*

Not only does God want to be our "happy thought" in those times of distress, fear and failure, but He also wants us to understand that we are *His* happy thought as well. Jeremiah 29:11 states this very clearly:

> For I know the thoughts that I think toward you, says the Lord, thoughts of peace and not of evil.
>
> —NKJV

The foundation for intimacy with God is the realization that we are His happy thought and that nothing we will ever say or do could change His mind about us. There is nothing you can do to cause God to love you any more than He does right now. There is nothing you can do to cause God to love you any less than He does right now.

I AM FATHER GOD'S HAPPY THOUGHT!

The following scriptures demonstrate how, in Christ, you are the "happy thought" of God and reveal His true character of love and forgiveness. As you meditate on these verses, allow the Holy Spirit to begin to transform your image of the Father into that of a loving Daddy who longs to care for you. You may even want to copy these verses and stick them on a mirror. Or better yet, memorize them!

- **My Father loves me with an everlasting love. I have never not been loved by my Father.**

I have loved you with an everlasting love; therefore I have drawn you with lovingkindness.

—JEREMIAH 31:3

- **My Father loves me so much that He gave His only Son to die for me so I might know His love.**

For God so loved the world, that He gave His only begotten Son, that whoever believes in Him should not perish, but have eternal life.

—JOHN 3:16

- **My Father loves me so much that He wants to express His love and affection to me.**

For the Father Himself loves you, because you have loved Me, and have believed that I came forth from the Father.

—JOHN 16:27

- **Nothing can separate me (not even my faults) from God's love for me.**

For I am convinced that neither death, nor life, nor angels, nor principalities, nor things present, nor things to come, nor powers, nor height, nor depth, nor any other created thing, shall be able to separate us from the love of God, which is in Christ Jesus our Lord.

—ROMANS 8:38–39

- **My Father loves me just as much as He loves His Son, Jesus.**

[I pray] that they may be perfected in unity, that the world may know that Thou didst send Me, and didst love them, even as Thou didst love Me.

—JOHN 17:23

- **Even when I have sinned, the Father loves me and asks me to sit beside Him with Christ.**

But God, being rich in mercy, because of His great love with which He loved us, even when we were dead in our transgressions, made us alive together with Christ (by grace you have been saved), and raised us up with Him, and seated us with Him in the heavenly places, in Christ Jesus.

—EPHESIANS 2:4–6

- **My Father wants me to overflow with His love.**

[I pray that you may] know the love of Christ which surpasses knowledge, that you may be filled up to all the fulness of God.

—EPHESIANS 3:19

- **Even when I am wounded, my Father sees me as beautiful and takes pleasure in me.**

For the LORD takes pleasure in His people; He will beautify the afflicted ones with salvation.

—PSALM 149:4

- **My Father's thoughts toward me are always good and filled with hope for me.**

"For I know the plans that I have for you," declares the LORD, "plans for welfare and not for calamity to give you a future and a hope."

—JEREMIAH 29:11

- **I am beautiful, handsome and pleasant in His eyes.**

"How beautiful you are, my darling, how beautiful you are! Your eyes are like doves."
   "How handsome you are, my beloved, and so pleasant."

—SONG OF SOLOMON 1:15–16

- **My love for Him fills Him with ecstasy and joy.**

How beautiful is your love, my sister, my bride! How much better is your love than wine.

—SONG OF SOLOMON 4:10

- **My Father is so pleased with my being His child that He will never leave me. He wants to meet all my needs.**

And he said to him, "My child, you have always been with me, and all that is mine is yours."

—LUKE 15:31

- **My Father likes being with me so much that He made His home with me.**

Jesus answered and said to him, "If anyone loves Me, he will keep My word; and My Father will love him, and We will come to him, and make Our abode with him."

—JOHN 14:23

- **I am to shine the light of the Father throughout the earth.**

You are the salt of the earth…You are the light of the world.

—MATTHEW 5:13–14

- **I am a witness of God to the world.**

But you shall receive power when the Holy Spirit has come upon you; and you shall be My witnesses both in Jerusalem, and in all Judea and Samaria, and even to the remotest part of the earth.

—ACTS 1:8

- **I am a minister of reconciliation for God.**

Now all these things are from God, who reconciled us to Himself through Christ, and gave us the ministry of reconciliation.

—2 CORINTHIANS 5:18

- **I am God's ambassador to the world.**

Therefore, we are ambassadors for Christ, as though God were entreating through us; we beg you on behalf of Christ, be reconciled to God.

—2 CORINTHIANS 5:20

- **I can do all things in Christ.**

I can do all things through Him who strengthens me.

—PHILIPPIANS 4:13

- **Jesus is not ashamed of me.**

For both He who sanctifies and those who are sanctified are all from one Father; for which reason He is not ashamed to call them brethren.

—HEBREWS 2:11

- **God is not ashamed to be my Father.**

Therefore God is not ashamed to be called their God; for He has prepared a city for them.

—HEBREWS 11:16

- **He has forgiven my iniquity and remembers my sin no more.**

"And they shall not teach again, each man his neighbor and each man his brother, saying, 'Know the LORD,' for they shall all know Me, from the least of them to the greatest of them," declares the LORD, "for I will forgive their iniquity, and their sin I will remember no more."

—JEREMIAH 31:34

- **He has put all of my sins under His feet and cast them into the depths of the sea.**

He will again have compassion on us; He will tread our enemies underfoot. Yes, Thou wilt cast all their sins into the depths of the sea.

—MICAH 7:19

- **God has redeemed me and forgiven all my sin.**

For He delivered us from the domain of darkness, and transferred us to the kingdom of His beloved Son, in whom we have redemption, the forgiveness of sins.

—COLOSSIANS 1:13–14

- **God forgives and cleanses me from all my sin.**

If we confess our sins, He is faithful and righteous to forgive us our sins and to cleanse us from all unrighteousness.

—1 JOHN 1:9

- **I am called a child of God.**

But as many as received Him, to them He gave the right to become children of God, even to those who believe in His name.

—JOHN 1:12

- **I am called Christ's friend.**

No longer do I call you slaves, for the slave does not know what his master is doing; but I have called you friends, for all things that I have heard from My Father I have made known to you.

—JOHN 15:15

- **In Christ it is just as if I had never sinned.**

Therefore having been justified by faith, we have peace with God through our Lord Jesus Christ.

—ROMANS 5:1

- **I belong to the Father.**

Do you not know that your body is a temple of the Holy Spirit who is in you, whom you have from God, and that you are not your own? For you have been bought with a price.

—1 CORINTHIANS 6:19–20

- **I have been adopted by the Father God.**

He predestined us to adoption as sons through Jesus Christ to Himself, according to the kind intention of His will.

—EPHESIANS 1:5

- **I am complete in Christ.**

In Him you have been made complete, and He is the head over all rule and authority.

—COLOSSIANS 2:10

- **I am free forever from condemnation.**

There is therefore now no condemnation for those who are in Christ Jesus. For the law of the Spirit of life in Christ Jesus has set you free from the law of sin and death.

—ROMANS 8:1–2

- **The Father is always for me, never against me.**

What then shall we say to these things? If God is for us, who is against us?

—Romans 8:31

- **Troubles do not separate me from God's love.**

Who shall separate us from the love of Christ? Shall tribulation, or distress, or persecution, or famine, or nakedness, or peril, or sword?

—Romans 8:35

- **I am hidden with Christ in the Father.**

For you have died and your life is hidden with Christ in God.

—Colossians 3:3

- **I am filled with power, love and a sound mind.**

For God has not given us a spirit of fear, but of power and of love and of a sound mind.

—2 Timothy 1:7, NKJV

- **I can find grace and mercy when I am hurting.**

Let us therefore draw near with confidence to the throne of grace, that we may receive mercy and may find grace to help in time of need.

—Hebrews 4:16

- **His perfect love casts out all fear.**

There is no fear in love; but perfect love casts out fear, because fear involves punishment, and the one who fears is not perfected in love.

—1 John 4:18

- **The evil one has no right to touch me while I am in my Father's arms.**

We know that no one who is born of God sins; but He who was born of God keeps him and the evil one does not touch him.

—1 JOHN 5:18

- **My Father wants to hold and comfort me when I'm afraid.**

For thus says the LORD, "Behold, I extend peace to her like a river, and the glory of the nations like an overflowing stream; and you shall be nursed, you shall be carried on the hip and fondled on the knees. As one whom his mother comforts, so I will comfort you; and you shall be comforted in Jerusalem."

—ISAIAH 66:12–13

- **God did not send His Son to die for me so that I might be judged by Him. When I believe in Him, I am not judged.**

For God did not send the Son into the world to judge the world; but that the world should be saved through Him. He who believes in Him is not judged; he who does not believe has been judged already, because he has not believed in the name of the only begotten Son of God.

—JOHN 3:17–18

- **The Father does not judge me.**

For not even the Father judges anyone, but He has given all judgment to the Son.

—JOHN 5:22

● **Jesus came to save me, not to judge me.**

And if anyone hears My sayings, and does not keep them, I do not judge him; for I did not come to judge the world, but to save the world.

—JOHN 12:47

The church would be powerfully transformed if God's people would saturate their minds in the truths of these simple verses. I hope you will meditate on them until you are *convinced* that the Father's love for you is great.

THE HEART OF THE FATHER

Several years ago, I was visiting my father in Florida, and we spent some time on the golf course. I was struggling with my swing when finally my dad handed me one of his clubs and said, "Try this. See how well you hit with it."

When I used that club, I hit the ball longer and straighter than I ever had before in my life. I understood why when I realized that the club my dad had handed to me had a $350 price tag! But when my father saw how well the club worked for me, he said without any hesitation whatsoever, "Take it, son. It's yours." It was in my father's heart to bless his son. I deserved it; I had been a good son for several years.

Of course, not too long after that, I took my son Micah out to the golf course to play with my new set of clubs. My son was nineteen and in a difficult, rebellious phase of life. That particular day he was playing very poorly, and although his dream was to one day play pro golf, on that day I was eating his lunch. Frustrated and angry, he began to complain, "You got those new Ping clubs. It's no wonder you're winning!" His attitude became worse and worse, until finally I got off the golf cart and switched my golf bag with his.

"Son, my clubs have become yours," I said to him. "You own them now. Do your best with them—that's all I ask."

Even though he had a miserable attitude and had done nothing to deserve my generosity, I gave him my brand-new set of golf clubs, worth almost a thousand dollars. I did it because it's in the heart of the father to bless his children. I wanted my son to be blessed, to have more and better things than myself in spite of his attitude.

That is also the nature of Father God. He sends rain on the just and the unjust. He blesses the deserving and the undeserving, simply because it is His character to love. Although He disciplines His children, the Father does not judge or condemn them (John 5:22). God is love, and everything He does is done in love (1 John 4:16). God is light, and in Him is no darkness at all (1 John 1:5). The loving thoughts of the Father toward us outnumber the sand; He considers us His precious children (Ps. 139:17–18). Love thinks no evil (1 Cor. 13:5, NKJV).

When you come to believe that you truly are Father's happy thought, you will be able to run freely to Him when you sin or when you experience times of distress. He will become your own happy thought because you have encountered firsthand His perfect love and acceptance, and His perfect love casts away all fear.

There are some who believe my views give people a license to sin. I did not realize they needed a license. It is the Law that arouses people's sinful passions (Rom. 7:5).

Others say that this theology makes God too common and lessens people's awe and fear of Him. May I ask you, Which Father would you have more respect for: the angry One or the loving, forgiving One? Which God does your family want to be most like? To which God would sinners be most attracted? With which God do you want to spend eternity?

If you have not found perfect peace and rest in Father God's unconditional love, then you may have a false image of who He is and what heaven will be like!

Father God, I come before You today and humbly ask You to forgive me for judging You wrongly and allowing misrepresentations of who You are to affect my perceptions of You. I have allowed religion that is based on performance and fear to color my thoughts toward You. I have sought to please You and gain Your acceptance through my good works. I thought You were angry with me and disappointed in me because I wasn't good enough to deserve Your love. My focus has been on religion instead of on my relationship with You. Please help me to gain a new understanding of Your unconditional love for me.

Now I bring to the cross of Jesus Christ all those who misrepresented to me Your character as a loving Father. I choose to forgive anyone who gave me a false impression of who You are. I understand now that You are not angry with me, but You are longing for deep fellowship with me because You love me so much. Help me to realize this fully and share it with everyone I meet. In Jesus' name, amen.

QUESTIONS FOR DISCUSSION

1. How were you disciplined by your father as a child? In what ways has this affected your image of your heavenly Father?

2. Think about the people you invite into your home. Are there some with whom you feel more comfortable than others? What is it about those people that allows you to relax in their presence? Are you "at home" with God when you spend time with Him, or are you on your best behavior, afraid to relax and be yourself? What would allow you to become more at home in the Father's presence?

3. Some Christians are afraid to approach God when they fall into sin and need His forgiveness. They may turn to religious activity to appease God's anger or commit further sins to drown out their feelings of guilt. After you have fallen into sin, what is your usual pattern of behavior?

4. When you are in trouble or distress, do you have a "happy thought" that brings you comfort? If so, what is it?

5. What misconceptions have you held about Father's thoughts toward you? How has the understanding that you are Father's happy thought changed those misconceptions?

Chapter Four

The Prodigal Father

W hen I was eighteen years old, my father gave me a haircut that changed my life. As a child, I didn't have a close relationship with my father. He was a strict military man, once a sergeant in the war, and that training and experience carried over into the way he related to his family. He loved us; there was no question that he would have given his own life for ours, but he also demanded obedience—unconditional and immediate—to his rules. These rules covered almost every area of our lives, right down to the way we wore our hair.

I was very young when I began to rebel against my father. Because there was no perceived love and intimacy to balance out the strictness of his discipline, by the age of twelve, I felt in my heart that I was no longer my father's son. Things got even worse as the years progressed until finally one day when I was eighteen years old, a serious incident took place that changed the course of our relationship.

Because of my father's military background, I was never allowed to grow my hair out long; I always had a flattop or crew cut. But when I was eighteen, my dad wasn't home much, so I decided to let my hair grow, hoping he wouldn't notice. Just as it had grown out enough to begin to touch the back of my collar, my dad came home one day and happened to notice my unruly locks. Immediately the command was issued, "You *will* have that hair cut off by tomorrow morning!"

In no uncertain terms that cannot be repeated in this book, I told my father what I thought of his rules and that I was absolutely not cutting off my hair.

I have never hit the floor so fast in my life, before or since! My father took me down and forcibly cut off my hair himself. He thought, mistakenly, that that was the best way to control the rebellion that was festering in my heart.

Unfortunately, his discipline had the opposite effect, and when I got up from the floor with considerably shorter hair, I called my father every name I could think of. Shortly after that I packed my bags and left my parents' house, essentially refusing to remain my father's son and severing all ties with him.

Not too long after leaving home, I got a job in a head shop (a place where they sold drug paraphernalia) on Main Street in Daytona Beach, Florida. It was the decade of the seventies, and this particular head shop, with its dark lighting and perpetual haze of drug-induced smoke, resembled a black cave. It was the place everyone went to smoke a joint and get stoned, and I joined in every chance I got.

But even though I had ceased being my father's son in my heart, he never ceased being my father in his. At that time, he was a mailman, and ironically, his route took him down Main Street every day, right past the head shop where I was "working" at getting stoned. Each time he passed by, he would come in, looking for his son. And each time he showed up, I went farther back into the cave to light up another joint. For over a year I rejected my father every single day.

But as wounded by my rejection as he was, my dad never stopped pursuing me. He knew where I was living—a communal home with several other hippies—and many times he came by and saw my motorcycle out front. He would stop, come to the front door and try to talk to me, but I would not receive him. In over a year, he had to have been rejected by me at least four hundred times, yet he continued to pursue me.

A broken, wounded father, whose last visible contact with his son had been an angry dispute culminating with his being called every name in the book, continued to seek a relationship with his son. If my earthly father, who had been so abused in his youth, had that depth of love and commitment to me, how much more does *Abba* Father, our heavenly Father who is perfect love, pursue restoration and intimacy with His wayward children?

WHO IS THE REAL PRODIGAL?

Eventually, my relationship with my father was restored, but only because of his relentless commitment to keep a relationship with his son. He was a prodigal father and a reflection to me of my heavenly Prodigal Father.

According to Webster's dictionary, the word *prodigal* means "one who spends or gives lavishly; recklessly extravagant."[1] When most people read the parable Jesus told in Luke 15, they refer to it as the story of the "Prodigal Son." Religion traditionally has made this story about the failure and sins of the son, just as religion often focuses more on the deeds of the sinner rather than focusing on what God has done to restore the relationship between Himself and His children. But this parable is more about a father's love and cry for intimacy than it is a son's rebellion. Although the son did spend his inheritance extravagantly, how much more recklessly did his father give compassion, forgiveness and grace to his son when he least deserved it?

> A certain man had two sons.
>
> —LUKE 15:11

This parable is a favorite story taught in churches and Sunday school classes, often to help demonstrate the love of the Father and teach the salvation message. But when Jesus began to tell this parable, it becomes clear from His very first sentence that He is not telling a story about how to become born again. The two sons in the parable were already members of their father's household, participating in a relationship with him and enjoying all the benefits of sonship. Instead of demonstrating how to begin a new relationship with the Father, Jesus wanted to teach a lesson about the restoration of a relationship with God that had already existed, a homecoming to the Father's love after the bond of intimacy had been broken by our self-love.

> And the younger of them said to his father, "Father, give me the share of the estate that falls to me." And he divided his wealth between them.
>
> —LUKE 15:12

The younger son did not value his relationship with his father for the companionship and intimacy that it offered. Instead, he became selfish and began to value his father for what material things he thought he was owed because of their relationship. Eventually he totally rejected any fellowship with his father in exchange for the balance of his inheritance. Immaturity only thinks of its own desires, not the heart of others.

In the culture of that day, a son's inheritance was not to come to him until the moment of his father's death. By asking for his inheritance early, this younger son was essentially saying, "Dad, I wish you were dead"—a complete, unspeakable insult at that time. The father was in no way required to give his son an early inheritance, and in fact, according to the Jewish law of that day, he could instead have given his son a one-way ticket to the local "rock concert"—a stoning as punishment for dishonoring his father.

But this father was different. He was a prodigal father, even before the son left. He gave his son the inheritance without anger or judgment, despite the son's greed and selfishness. He had already forgiven his son for his rebellion, or he would never have given him the inheritance.

DEMANDING GOD'S INHERITANCE

During the 1980s and early 1990s many Christians began to value God for what they could receive and what He would do in their lives and not for intimacy and love. Many began to hear about healing, so thousands would flock to crusades to receive that blessing from the Lord. Then, a different manifestation of power would begin in another church, and thousands would flock there to receive that portion of their perceived inheritance. For some, chasing after one demonstration of God's power or another became more important than fostering an intimate relationship with the Father and His love transforming their families.

An attitude began to fester among many of these Christians that God somehow owed them the benefits of healing and financial prosperity because it was part of their inheritance in Christ, but they did not pursue the way of love. Many ministers began to compare themselves to each other; seeing the power and favor of God in some ministries, others became caught up in ambition, pride or jealousy. They wanted the same power of God to be displayed in their own ministries, not in order to bless the people, but to receive the honor and favor that such ministers seemed to have.

Because of His love and grace, the Father still pours out His blessings even under these circumstances, but when His children continue to value Him for what He can do for them, they miss out on the greatest blessing of all—an intimate relationship with Him. When the younger son only thought about his own desires and needs, he was demonstrating his immaturity. Often, immature Christians seek the blessings of their relationship with God rather than hungering for God Himself, but this attitude, if continued long enough, will eventually lead us into a distant land, just as the younger son found himself far from home and away from his father's protection and care.

> And not many days later, the younger son gathered everything together and went on a journey into a distant country, and there he squandered his estate with loose living.
>
> —LUKE 15:13

It was not long after the son began to devalue the relationship that he had with his father that he left his father's house and began to pursue his fleshly lusts. There was a definite point when he left and assumed control of his own life. And it was at that point that his father was no longer able to offer him the benefits of being his child. He remained the father's son, but was no longer covered by the father's house.

We must identify that point in our own lives—the point at which we say, "I want to do this myself. I want to control this on my own. God, give me what You owe me and then let me do things my own way." As soon as we reach that point, we begin drifting away from the Father's embrace, and sooner or later we will end up consuming the blessings that He sends us on our own lusts.

Throughout the 1980s and early 1990s, many took the inheritance of God but did not seek His heart for intimacy. There were times when we demanded the blessings from God—healing, the gifts of the Spirit, His power demonstrated in signs and wonders—and in His graciousness, God did give us what we asked for. But the end result was an eventual drought in the spiritual life of the church. When our attitude was that of "gimme, gimme, gimme," we were outside of an intimate relationship with the Father, and the door was opened for competition, strife, division, lust and every evil work to enter.

In a 1998 interview with Rick Knoth, managing editor of the Assemblies of God *Enrichment Journal*, Promise Keepers founder and president Bill McCartney stated that they had researched and found that 62 percent of Christian men admitted to struggles with sexual sin—pornography, adultery and sensuality.[2] How could this be? When Christians value the Father more for what He can do for them than for intimacy and love, they eventually begin to seek to fulfill their own selfish desires rather than enjoy the relationship they have with God. Then, in order to fill the void that has been created, they may begin to pursue one or more counterfeit affections—passions of the flesh, power, possessions or position. This vicious cycle can continue until they realize that what they are lusting for will not satisfy them, until they recognize that they have an unmet need for love and intimacy that only the Father's embrace can fulfill.

> Now when he had spent everything, a severe famine occurred in that country, and he began to be in need.
>
> —LUKE 15:14

When we leave the Father's house and begin drifting away from an intimate relationship with Him, it is time to heed the still, small voice within: "Warning! You are about to step in it! You are about to hurt the people around you! Warning! Warning!" If we don't take caution at that point, we may fall into the trap of counterfeit affections. Looking for the lost intimacy that had been so prevalent in the Father's house, we may seek to replace it with a false sense of intimacy derived from pornography, addictions, compulsions or sexual perversion. It may start with just a thought, but if left unchecked, it can lead to an outright bondage of addiction that leaves us wallowing in the defilement of the pigpen, feeling dirty and ashamed.

LIFE IN THE PIGPEN

> And he went and attached himself to one of the citizens of that country, and he sent him into his fields to feed swine. And he was longing to fill his stomach with the pods that the swine were eating, and no one was giving anything to him.
>
> —LUKE 15:15–16

The end result of the younger son's departure from his father's house was the ultimate degradation in the culture of that time: life in the pigpen, a complete abomination for a Jewish son. Even worse, the fate of the swine was better than the state the son was in; he was actually jealous of the pigs because they had more to fill their cravings than he did!

How do well-meaning children of the Father fall into such unclean states? I have spent the last fourteen years ministering to wounded ministers and their wives. Rarely a week goes by that I do not find myself talking with someone in ministry who has found him or herself involved in an immoral situation, and not a one of them had planned on drifting into that sin. They were all men and women who had been hungry for God and committed to serving Him in ministry. But every day disappointments and unmet expectations can cause even the most well-meaning Christians to lose their sense of love and intimacy with the Father, and eventually they drift away from the Father's embrace and straight to the place they said they would never go. The pigpen, that place of shame and self-condemnation, becomes their new home until they recognize that where they are truly longing to be, the only place where their needs will ultimately be met, is back in their Father's embrace.

Your spouse cannot ultimately meet your need for intimacy. If you are expecting him or her to give you all the love that you need, when they are unable to do so, you will be vulnerable to being defiled by someone else with an unmet love need. The kind of sacrificial love that a marriage requires can only flow out of the love that comes from the Father's embrace, from a relationship first established with God, from abundantly receiving His love and then giving it away to your spouse. Until you value intimacy and love more than what God can do for you, you will continue to have a void in your heart. And, as in the laws of nature, wherever there is a void, something will try to fill it. Some people try to fill this void with alcohol, with drugs or even with religion. But the longing and emptiness in your heart cannot be filled by anyone or anything except for a relationship with the Father that is built upon love and intimacy and not duty and works. Until you have experienced this, it may be difficult to experience a truly intimate relationship with another person.

COME TO YOUR SENSES!

When you have hit rock bottom and are in the midst of the pigpen of shame and despair, a homecoming begins when you start to remember what a loving and compassionate Father you have. In the midst of his sin, the younger son began to remember how things had been when he lived in his father's house:

> But when he came to his senses, he said, "How many of my father's hired men have more than enough bread, but I am dying here with hunger! I will get up and go to my father, and will say to him, 'Father, I have sinned against heaven, and in your sight; I am no longer worthy to be called your son; make me as one of your hired men.'"
> —LUKE 15:17–19

The son finally realized his error, and his motives went from "gimme, gimme" to "change me, change me." Change anything that is not comfortable with love. He remembered that even though he had completely forsaken his father, his father would never forsake him. True repentance involves both a change of heart and a change in actions. This younger son's heart attitude was changed from selfishness to a brokenness and humility as he realized that no matter how much he failed, his father would be waiting for him with outstretched arms. And then he determined to take action, to get up from the pigpen of shame and take the steps necessary to return to his father's house.

> And he got up and came to his father. But while he was still a long way off, his father saw him, and felt compassion for him, and ran and embraced him, and kissed him.
> —LUKE 15:20

What love this prodigal father had for his son! What love our heavenly Father has for us! Before the son had ever left home, his father had already forgiven him. The love he had for his son was not based upon the son's behavior. He was simply waiting for his son to return so that he could fully express his affectionate love.

Before you even take one step outside of the covering of your heavenly Father, He has already forgiven you. Paul has told us that even "if we are faithless, He remains faithful; for He cannot deny Himself" (2 Tim. 2:13). Not only will He forgive you, but He will also run to you as soon as you take one step back toward His love. He reminds us in Jeremiah 31:3, "I have loved you with an everlasting love; therefore I have drawn you with lovingkindness." It is the Father who is prodigal, whose love is recklessly extravagant, who is ready to pour out undeserved blessings, grace and mercy on our lives.

> And the son said to him, "Father, I have sinned against heaven and in your sight; I am no longer worthy to be called your son." But the father said to his slaves, "Quickly bring out the best robe and put it on him, and put a ring on his hand and sandals on his feet; and bring the fattened calf, kill it, and let us eat and be merry; for this son of mine was dead, and has come to life again; he was lost, and has been found."
>
> —LUKE 15:21–24

When we have failed, the Father runs to us with His arms outstretched, ready to welcome us back into His embrace with all of the fullness of His forgiveness and love, but sometimes our own attitude can hold us back. The shame of what we have done, the embarrassment of our failures, still lingers, even after we experience God's forgiveness. "I am no longer worthy to be called your son," the son, not the father, declared. But not only did the father accept him back as a full member of his household, but he also gave him the royal treatment! He put the father's *best* robes upon him, the ring of inheritance upon his hand and sandals that only sons wore upon his feet. He rejoiced that his long-lost, beloved son had returned.

FIG LEAVES OF SHAME

Many children of God are living under the burden of condemnation from past sins they may have committed. They are playing the shame game, a cycle that began at the time of the very first sin in the Garden of Eden. When a Christian falls into sin, there is an immediate sense of failure, of not measuring up to God's expectations. That failure leads to shame and embarrassment for not being perfect and guilt for having violated God's law. Shame and guilt lead to fear—fear of being found out, fear of rejection, fear of God's wrath—and the natural reaction to fear is to hide.

When Adam and Eve sinned in the Garden of Eden, they were caught in this cycle, which culminated in their hide-and-seek game with God (Gen. 3:7–10). Their shame and embarrassment caused them to sew fig leaves together to hide their nakedness. Today, Christians do not use literal fig leaves to hide their sin from God, but they may use hyperreligious activity, or spiritual fig leaves, to cover themselves. These can be expressed in the acrostic FIG LEAF:[3]

> **F** ear
>
> **I** nsecurity
>
> **G** uilt
>
> **L** oneliness
>
> **E** scapism
>
> **A** nxiety
>
> **F** ailure

> **F**—When Christians fail, they begin to experience *fear*. They may fear rejection by God or by other Christians who may discover what they have done. They may begin to fear intimacy, because to allow themselves to be fully known would involve disclosing their imperfections, or they may fear further failure, which can paralyze them and render them incapable of moving ahead in intimacy with God.

> **I**—When these fears take root in their hearts, they often become *insecure*, insecure with God, with themselves and in their relationships with others.

> **G**—*Guilt* is the natural consequence of unconfessed sin.

Until true repentance occurs, we may be hounded by guilt and self-condemnation.

L—Not being at home in the Father's love brings a sense of *loneliness* and isolation, for one cannot experience true intimacy in any relationship when sin and shame are in the way.

E—Unable to experience the love of the Father or intimacy with others may cause us to turn to *escapism*, seeking comfort wherever it can be found, becoming addicted to movies, video games, romance novels, alcohol, drugs or pornography. Some Christians may even escape into excessive religious activity, focusing on doing things for God and thinking that their aggressive striving will earn a place back to the Father's heart.

A—If we are not at peace, resting in the love of our Father, we cannot avoid a lifestyle of *anxiety*. When there is unresolved sin in a person's heart, anxiety will simmer just below the surface until the root cause is dealt with.

F—All of these consequences of sin create a vicious cycle, causing further *failure* to take place.

But if we turn our hearts toward the Father's house, He will run toward us and welcome us back into His embrace. He exchanges our fig leaves of shame for royal robes of righteousness. He places His ring back on our finger, restoring us to the place of full sonship in His household.

SIX STEPS TO AN INTIMATE RELATIONSHIP WITH THE FATHER

How does a homecoming take place? This parable demonstrates six simple steps we can take to restore the relationship of intimacy with the Father that was lost through our valuing the Father for what He can do for us and not for intimacy and love.

1. Come to your right senses.

If you have received Christ as your Savior, you are a son or daughter of the Father of creation. Even if you are living in a pigpen of impurity and sin, understand that is not where you belong. Come to your senses! Your Father loves you and is eagerly awaiting your return to His house. If you are afraid to approach an angry God who is pointing His finger of judgment in your face, you don't have an accurate understanding of God's love. The younger son realized that he had a prodigal father, one who loved him unconditionally and who couldn't wait to welcome him home.

2. Confess your sin.

Declare as the rebellious son declared, "I have sinned against heaven and in your eyes." His attitude changed from one of self-love to one of humility. Jesus tells us that we must humble ourselves and become like little children in order to enter God's kingdom, and that "whoever then humbles himself as [a] child, he is the greatest in the kingdom of heaven" (Matt. 18:4). There will be no homecoming without humility, but when we humble ourselves in repentance, we will be exalted into the Father's presence.

3. Forgive your earthly father (or mother) for any hurts or issues of the past.

Our earthly parents are only human, and they are bound to make mistakes. Often these mistakes color our later views of God and affect our ability to perceive Him as a loving and forgiving heavenly Father. By practicing a lifestyle of forgiveness and releasing your parents to God, you will actually free yourself from your past and begin a journey of experiencing unhindered intimacy with God. This is the Father's embrace.

4. See the Father's house as your source of love.

The lifestyle of the pigpen could not meet the needs of the discontent son. Even with the inheritance he had received, he was still left wanting when he lacked a relationship with his father. You will not find true fulfillment in counterfeit affections, no matter how appealing they may seem at first. Don't expect your husband or wife, your career, hobbies or religious activities to satisfy you if you aren't also fostering an intimate relationship with God that is evidenced by intimate relationships with others.

5. Anticipate the Father's embrace.

Most Christians expect the rod of judgment when they fail. Even if they do summon up the courage to approach God with their sin, they do so while cringing in fear or shame. But they don't realize that their deepest moment of failure is when the Father most desires their homecoming. He grieves for their pain, and His compassion is endless. He is waiting with open arms to embrace His wayward sons and daughters as they return to Him.

6. Return to the presence of the Father.

The spirit of adoption was released over you when you were born again (Rom. 8:15). You became God's child, and He will not deny His name that was stamped on you through Christ. The prodigal Father eagerly awaits your return. He is waiting for you to exchange your fig leaves of shame and for His love to cover your sin (1 Pet. 4:8).

When I was living with the hippies in the commune after leaving my parents' house, I rejected my father day after day after day. But he was relentless in his pursuit of the son whom he loved.

One night, at 2:30 A.M., the phone rang in my father's house. My dad answered and heard the words he had dreaded for months: "Mr. Frost, we have your son here at the hospital." I had taken an overdose of "orange sunshine," the LSD of choice at that time. For five days, I lay in a drugged, semicomatose state; the doctors could do nothing for me but wait to see whether my brain would come out of it. My father never left my side, and I miraculously recovered with no permanent damage. The only thing I remember in those five days is hearing my dad say over and over again, "Son, I love you. Everything's going to be all right."

My father had never been able to embrace me or say the words "I love you." Yet when I failed him the most, it was at that time he expressed the love that I had need of so much. As wounded as my earthly father was, and at the time when I had brought the greatest pain, failure and shame to his life, he still forgave me and actively sought to restore our relationship. How much more do you think your heavenly Father pursues you and longs to welcome you back into His loving embrace? Hear the words He is whispering to you: *My child, I love you. Return to Me. Everything is going to be all right.*

Pray this prayer in response to the Father's heart:

> *Dear heavenly Father, thank You for Your love that surpasses my understanding. I long to return to Your house. I confess my sin. Please forgive me for valuing my inheritance and the things I hope to gain for myself more than I value an intimate relationship with You. I have taken my inheritance and consumed it on my own lusts. I took from You what You were so willing to give to me, and I have not been faithful with it. I have left Your house to pursue my own selfish interests, but now I long to return to You. I make a choice to leave the pigpen of sin and shame. Let me experience Your compassion. Run to me and welcome me back as Your child in Your loving embrace. Restore me to Your love. In Jesus' name, amen.*

QUESTIONS FOR DISCUSSION

1. The younger son demanded his inheritance—what he felt his father owed him—and then left his father's house. Have you ever valued what God could do *for you* more than you valued a relationship of love and intimacy *with Him*? What was the end result of this attitude?

2. Have you ever gone through a "pigpen experience"? Describe the moment in which you "came to your senses."

3. What are some of the fig leaves that you hide behind after you have sinned? How can you relinquish these patterns to God and stop participating in the "shame game"?

SECTION TWO

HINDRANCES TO EXPERIENCING THE FATHER'S LOVE

For I am convinced that neither death, nor life, nor angels, nor principalities, nor things present, nor things to come, nor powers, nor height, nor depth, nor any other created thing, shall be able to separate us from the love of God, which is in Christ Jesus our Lord.

—ROMANS 8:38–39

We have seen in the previous chapters how the hour has come when God is now revealing Himself to the world as a loving and gentle Father. When pursuing an experiential encounter with the Father's love, it is difficult to process His love as fast as you want because there are often barriers (hindrances) that will slow you down. Pride, counterfeit affections, hidden core pain from the past, unforgiveness, unresolved conflicts, shame, judgmentalism and aggressive striving are some of the major hindrances. Often, as Christians, we think that we have put all these issues behind us. The following chapters will help to bring deeper revelation and light to some of the primary issues that may slow you down in receiving a deep experience in the Father's healing love.

The Father desires that His love begin to lift you above the circumstances that have held you back from experiencing intimacy and love. As you read through these chapters, remember that a river always flows to the lowest point. It flows to those who have been deeply wounded by the sins of others and to those whose own sins have left them clothed with guilt and shame. It flows most freely to those who are meek and lowly of heart and who will come to the Father like a little child in need of a daddy's comforting love.

> He has regarded the prayer of the destitute, and has not despised their prayer... For He looked down from His holy height; from heaven the Lord gazed upon the earth, to hear the groaning of the prisoner; to set free those who were doomed to death.
>
> —PSALM 102:17, 19–20

> Then some children were brought to Him so that He might lay His hands on them and pray; and the disciples rebuked them. But Jesus said, "*Let the children alone, and do not hinder them from coming to Me; for the kingdom of heaven belongs to such as these.*"
>
> —MATTHEW 19:13–14, EMPHASIS ADDED

Chapter Five

The Older Brother Syndrome, or the Son Willing to Become a Slave

I n 722 B.C., God's people, the nation of Israel, were finally taken into captivity by the wicked, degenerate nation of Assyria. Before that time, they had been threatened for years and years by this, their most dreaded of enemies. During this time one of the greatest illustrations of repentance and turning to the Lord took place that is recorded in the Old Testament. The Assyrians were some of the most depraved people on the planet at that time. They were a race of unrepentant idolaters, sexual fornicators and ruthless murderers—a bloodthirsty and savage people who sacrificed their own children to false gods and who took pleasure in tyrannizing the nations they conquered.

As He often does, God dealt with the situation in an unexpected way—He appointed His prophet Jonah to travel to Nineveh, the capital city of Assyria, and call the people there, essentially Jonah's enemies, to repentance. Of course, Jonah's refusal and subsequent disobedience in fleeing to Tarshish has made him a rather infamous character in our Sunday school classes. But the story of Jonah doesn't end when he had his not-so-surprising change of heart in the belly of the fish. After he was spit back up onto the beach, he did follow God's command and became the first missionary to the people of Nineveh.

Unfortunately, Jonah's motives in pursuing this ministry weren't altogether pure. Jonah never wanted his mission to Nineveh to be successful. He proudly strode through the city streets, loudly proclaiming, "Yet forty days and Nineveh will be overthrown" (Jon. 3:4). But the king and the people of Nineveh heeded Jonah's message. To his utter displeasure, they dressed themselves in sackcloth and ashes, declared a fast of repentance and began to cry out to God for mercy. Jonah believed God would spare Nineveh, but he lacked the compassion for the people that God had (Jon. 4:1–2).

The heart of the Father is always responsive to those who truly turn to Him, no matter how far from Him they have strayed or how wicked and depraved they might be. God relented from the catastrophe that He had planned for the Assyrians. Instead, He forgave the people of Nineveh and welcomed them into His presence.

One would think that Jonah would have been pleased to see his ministry succeed. But Jonah was suffering from the "older brother syndrome." After Nineveh's repentance, he threw a colossal pity party, becoming angry because God was not going to punish the Assyrians in the way he felt they deserved. As Jonah was pouting outside of the city, God caused a plant to grow over his head and provide him with shade. This small convenience seemed to brighten Jonah's mood immediately—that is, until the plant died and the sun once again beat down ferociously on Jonah's head. His pity party resumed and then grew until Jonah became virtually suicidal, begging God to take his life. Jonah thought his anger was justified, but God's response to him demonstrates the compassion the Father has for all people and His desire for the lost to come home:

> You had compassion on the plant for which you did not work, and which you did not cause to grow, which came up overnight and perished overnight. And should I not have compassion on Nineveh, the great city in which there are more than 120,000 persons who do not know the difference between their right and left hand, as well as many animals?
>
> —JONAH 4:10–11

The Bible doesn't tell us Jonah's response to God's reprimand. We can only hope that he recognized that his attitude was wrong and experienced a homecoming of his own with the Father. But the question for us to ponder is this: When God wanted to bring revival to the most wicked city on earth, with whom did He have more trouble, the people of Nineveh or the man of God sent to that city? We may think that revival only comes when the hearts of the sinners turn to God, but the hearts of Christian leaders must also be prepared.

Jonah was exhibiting the older brother syndrome that we may have when we see God bestow His blessing on those who we feel don't deserve it. These sins of the older brother may in reality be a greater hindrance to the kingdom of God than are the sins of the younger son. While the younger brother may commit sins of immorality and violate God's laws of behavior, the older brother commits the greatest sin of all, the sin against love.

In the last chapter, we discovered that the younger son in actuality has a compassionate, forgiving father waiting to welcome him home with open arms. But the younger son too often has an older brother also waiting for him back in the father's house with a not-so-welcoming attitude. What would have happened to the younger son if the older brother had approached him before the compassionate father did?

THE SIN AGAINST LOVE

The final chapter of the parable of the prodigal father demonstrates where many Christians can be found, especially many who are involved in ministry. They may be the most loyal, hard-working and dutiful workers in their service to the Lord. From all outward appearances, they seem to be the holiest, most virtuous members of the church, but a closer examination of their hearts tells a different story. Jealousy, anger, pride, spiritual ambition, self-righteousness and sullenness are often lurking just below the surface in these souls that lack an experiential revelation of the Father's love. Many have the attitude of the older brother, the good son, and their sin against love can misrepresent the Father's heart in far greater ways than the more blatant sins of the rebellious son.

> Now his older son was in the field, and when he came and approached the house, he heard music and dancing. And he summoned one of the servants and began inquiring what these things might be. And he said to him, "Your brother has come, and your father has killed the fattened calf, because he has received him back safe and sound."
>
> But he became angry, and was not willing to go in; and his father came out and began entreating him. But he answered and said to his father, "Look! For so many years I have been serving you, and I have never neglected a command of yours; and yet you have never given me a kid, that I might be merry with my friends; but when this son of yours came, who has devoured your wealth with harlots, you killed the fattened calf for him."
>
> And he said to him, "My child, you have always been with me, and all that is mine is yours. But we had to be merry and rejoice, for this brother of yours was dead and has begun to live, and was lost and has been found."
>
> —LUKE 15:25–32

The father's heart was full of compassion for the son who had left his house and then returned in humility and repentance. But the older brother sulked in jealousy outside of the father's house when he saw the party that was being thrown for his brother. His attitude put a damper on the entire celebration; it threatened to affect the happiness of the younger brother, the father and all of the guests.

How many wayward children would like to return to the house of the Father but are prevented from experiencing a true homecoming because of the unloving attitudes of those within the church? Those who profess to love the Lord and who diligently live by a strict form of law and legalism are sometimes the greatest hindrance to the advancement of the kingdom of God. Sins of disposition can be worse than sins of behavior, not because one sin is necessarily greater than another, but because of what the sins of disposition reveal: a lack of experiencing the Father's love at the very root of the soul.

This sin against love may be the greatest sin a person can commit because it violates the very nature of the kingdom of love that God is seeking to establish on the earth. Yet ironically, that is the sin that many Christians, and even many ministers of the gospel, drift toward, the sin of aggressively striving to be better than others and earn their way to favor with God. It is so easy for us to judge the offenses of the rebellious son, to identify and condemn them, because those offenses are more obvious to the outside observer. But the older brother looks so righteous, so good, that it is often difficult to discern the hidden sins that lurk within his heart.

The attitude of the father toward the older brother is the same as the attitude he has toward the younger son: His loving compassion entreats him to change his attitude and join in the party. The older brother has left the father's house just as surely as the younger son left, and the father realizes that both of his sons need a homecoming. The younger son had lived in a distant land, but the heart of the older brother was much more distant from home. He had slaved faithfully in the fields for many years, living under the father's roof, but he never really knew him—he had never cultivated an intimate relationship with his dad. But the father still entreats him to come home, to change his attitude and join in the joyous celebration.

When I first came into the Father's house, my heart was filled with so much joy and love that I wanted to spread it to everyone I met. I was a rebellious son who had entered into the welcoming embrace of Father God, and I experienced the joyous homecoming salvation found in Jesus Christ. At that time, I was living on the sea between twenty and twenty-five days out of the month, and it was just God and me out under the stars. I didn't know anything at all about the Christian lifestyle; all I knew was that I longed to spend time in the presence of my Father. I would weep for hours, overwhelmed by His love and forgiveness. I realized that I wanted to share this overwhelming love with others, so I decided to become a minister. I left the life of the sea and enrolled in a traditional Bible school to learn all the things I needed to know about ministry.

I soon began to drift further and further into the attitude of the older brother. In Bible school, I began to learn the disciplines of the Christian faith: prayer, the study of the Word, witnessing and evangelism, fasting and tithing. I began to slave faithfully in the fields of the Father, and I was always striving to live up to my own exacting standards. I never allowed one moral failure in my behavior, not one slip-up or negligence of integrity in my actions.

I became so proficient in every task I was given in Bible school that when I finally graduated and was sent out into the ministry, I was immediately given the position of a senior pastor. I quickly learned how to please the governing board of my denomination: grow the membership of my congregation and increase the financial income of my church. By my second year in the ministry, I had the fastest-growing church in my denominational district. At the annual pastors' conference, I was brought to the platform and given a plaque for my service. By all outward appearances, I had become a success in the ministry. But my heart told a different story. I was gradually becoming more distant from the Father, and I was drifting away from the joy of my salvation bit by bit, day by day.

When we begin to serve God for what we can receive from our service, no matter how great the call of God is on our lives, no matter how powerful the gifts or the anointing flow in our ministry, that underlying attitude of self-love can begin to produce a hidden resentment and anger, fueled by a fear of rejection and a fear of failure. As soon as our service is no longer motivated by love but by a need to be needed or seen, we begin to drift away from the Father's heart of compassion, and we will soon find ourselves in the older brother's shoes, slaving in the fields and thinking all along that we dwell in His house of love.

There is nothing wrong with practicing the Christian disciplines of tithing, fasting, prayer, Bible study or witnessing. These are necessary, and they should be the noticeable, outward expressions of the intimate relationship that we are cultivating with our heavenly Father. But as I was learning these disciplines in a rigid holiness environment, I was filtering them through the system of love that I had learned in my childhood. When I was younger, I had to strive to receive any type of affirmation from my father. I had to hit the ball just right. I had to get straight As on my report card. I had to be the perfect, obedient son. However, my obedience was based on the fear of failure and the fear of rejection. I obeyed my father in order to gain his approval rather than obeying him because of the close relationship that I had with him and a desire not to grieve him.

That striving attitude carried over into my relationship with God when I began to learn the "rules" of the Christian walk. The Christian disciplines, when motivated by unconditional love, can bring great blessings to the church and be an important witness to those outside of the faith. But when they were poured through the filter system that I had carried over from my childhood, they created a burden too heavy for me to bear. No amount of fasting or tithing or servitude can earn the love of the Father, especially when the motivation behind these actions is based on a desire for personal gain and reward.

As the weight of pleasing the Father became heavier and heavier on my shoulders, I sought release from the burden by looking down on others not as disciplined as I was in order to make me look good. I spent a great deal of time and energy on achieving excellence in myself, and I came to expect that same level of commitment from my family, my congregation and everyone else around me. When I placed my exacting standards on other people and found them to be lacking, my own ego was inflated and my spirituality seemed that much more holy, more pious and more perfect than theirs. But I never sought the self-deception that I was in.

SLAVING IN THE FIELDS: A VICIOUS CYCLE

The older brother syndrome creates its own cycle that takes the sincere but gullible participant down a subtle path of destruction that, if left unchecked, ultimately leads to a cold heart void of love, tenderness or compassion. The key to breaking the cycle is to recognize the symptoms early enough to thwart its development. The sins of the older brother can cause severe damage in the church if allowed to continue, because the sins against love and compassion are the most harmful to needy people seeking for forgiveness and healing. It is a great tragedy when wayward younger brothers and sisters who are on the verge of repentance and restoration to the Father are shut out by the self-righteousness of those who profess the name of Christ.

As soon as the older brother or good son drifts away from the Father's house because of a negative attitude of self-love, jealousy or judgmentalism, an *emotional and spiritual distance* is immediately created between him and his Father. Any distance from God's love will gradually gravitate to law and legalism, and it will lead to *feelings of insecurity*, because it is the unconditional acceptance of the Father that gives us our true value and self-worth. Deeply intimate relationships with other people are only possible between individuals who are secure in God's love, because the foundation of such relationships is love, trust and commitment. As soon as distance from God and insecurity begin to occur, intimacy with others becomes very difficult because we treat others in the way we feel about ourselves.

The second step in the cycle takes place when the person tries to regain the intimacy that has been lost by *aggressively striving* to gain the acceptance and approval of others. The older brother was driven to slave in his father's fields to earn his position in the family; what he didn't realize was that his position was already secure, no matter what he accomplished in life.

When a person believes that his value is based on his performance and what others, including God, think of him, it leads directly to the third step: *competition.* He must become better than anyone else in order to receive the Father's love. When a minister reaches this stage, he can become overly concerned with the church across the street or how his own ministry measures up when compared with the other ministries in town.

When we are more concerned with the opinions of other people than with what God thinks, we start drifting away from intimacy with Him. In Isaiah 51, God declares:

> I, even I, am He who comforts you. Who are you that you are afraid of man who dies, and of the son of man who is made like grass; that you have forgotten the LORD your Maker, who stretched out the heavens, and laid the foundations of the earth…
>
> —ISAIAH 51:12–13

When the comparison to others comes up short, as it eventually will, the inevitable result is *envy*, the fourth step in the vicious cycle. Unhealthy competition leads to feelings of ill will toward those in the same line of work. Not everyone can receive the plaque for the fastest-growing church, but most want it. The real problem comes when we believe that to truly be accepted, or important in life, we must be the one to earn it. If we aren't able to achieve what we believe we must, we may begin to *judge ourselves*, the fifth step in the cycle. And finally, because of the guilt that we feel for coming up short, we put on a cloak of *defensiveness*, and the need to be right becomes more important than fostering healthy relationships.

This final step seals the hardness of heart of the older brother. Most older brothers are right; they are usually the most loyal, hardest-working, best performers in the church. But often they would rather prove their righteousness than promote intimate relationships. They value obedience over relationship, and they use that self-righteousness to justify their negative attitudes. At that point, other people begin to feel devalued: The family suffers first, then the church and other members of the body of Christ. And sadly, this attitude of the older brother keeps younger or rebellious sons from returning to the Father, perhaps the worst consequence of all.

When I was deeply entrenched in this cycle, the affirmation of men was the most important thing in the world to me, even more important than pointing repentant sinners back to God and creating an atmosphere of love and grace at home. I felt more like a servant in the Father's fields than a son who lived at rest in the Father's house. Jack Winter wrote in his book *The Homecoming*, "Servants can only *bring* others to a master. Sons are the ones who can *point* others to their Father."[1]

My servitude led to a legalistic attitude that prevented my family and friends from being close to me. I valued their immediate and unconditional obedience more than I valued an intimate relationship with them. My children were even afraid to bring their own friends over to our house because of my strict standards. But when God began to work on my heart, I had a revelation of the love of the Father, and things began to change in our family.

About six months after my change of heart, my daughter called from school, asking if she could bring a friend home. I was surprised, because before I had a revelation of love, my children dared not bring friends home. I readily agreed, until she said, "Well, Dad, I just need to prepare you…"

"Prepare me for what, Sarah?"

"Well, her name is Erica, and she has orange hair."

That took me aback, but I composed myself and replied, "That's fine, honey. Just bring her on home."

"But that's not all, Dad. She's also got a cat collar around her arm."

"A what?"

"And she's got earrings in strange places."

"Why do you want to bring this girl into our house, Sarah?"

My daughter's answer surprised me and showed me how much God had changed my heart. "Because she's so hurt. Her own father is a drug addict and left her family years ago. I want her to meet you, Dad. I want her to see what having a loving and tender father is like."

Of course, I welcomed Erica into our home. At first, she was sullen and angry. She sat on my couch with her arms crossed as I tried to carry on a conversation with her. I talked with her about her parents and told her about my own childhood and how I had left my parents' house and built a tough shell around my heart, just as she had. I didn't even mention the name of Jesus to her; Sarah and I just sat next to her, and eventually I was able to hold her hand as a father would hold the hand of his own daughter. I watched as the Holy Spirit melted her heart. When I told her how I had wounded my own daughter for years because of the hurts I had experienced in my own life and then asked if I could stand in as her dad and ask her to forgive me for rejecting her, she began to cry. I never brought up the subject of God, but when it was time for her to go, she asked if she could return to our home.

When she and Sarah came into the house the next day, I heard Sarah call out, "Dad, where are you?" And right after that, I heard Erica's voice, "Dad, I'm home." For six weeks, Erica was a daily guest in our home, and each week, something changed in her appearance. Her natural hair color returned, the collar and earrings in strange places disappeared, and eventually Erica gave her heart to Christ. Erica was led home to the Father because I had relinquished the attitude of the older brother and instead was motivated by love and compassion for a lost and hurting little girl.

Bad people loved to hang out with Jesus. Good people wanted to kill Him.

THE LOVE OF THE LAW OR THE LAW OF LOVE

Any Christian discipline that you practice, any theology that you hold, if it is not rooted and grounded in the love of the Father, will gradually cause you to gravitate toward the love of the law. This legalism may have disastrous consequences: Lives may be destroyed, ministries may be lost, and revivals may be quenched because of the sin of the older brother. Today God is dealing with the hearts of ministers and Christian leaders, with those who profess to love Him and follow His ways, to return to Him and experience a homecoming, just as His wayward children experience.

Do you notice any of the symptoms of the older brother syndrome in your heart or ministry? Are you aggressively striving to gain the approval of God or other people? Do you find yourself constantly competing to be the best in your career or in your service to God at the cost of dishonoring or devaluing others? Do you require perfection in those around you and mete out a judgmental or a condemning attitude when this perfection is not achieved? Do you have a greater love of the law than you do of the needs of people? If so, you may be cultivating the attitude of the older brother, and you are in need of a homecoming with your Father.

Until I let go of the striving, jealousy and rivalry in my heart, I led a life of frustration and resentment. No promotion was ever enough. No acknowledgment or accolade would completely satisfy. The success of others would frustrate me, and my feelings of servitude only increased as I moved further and further from dwelling in the Father's embrace.

The love of God is a gift, free and undeserved. There is nothing you can do to be loved by Him any more than you already are. And there is nothing you can do to lessen His love. God's love is unconditional, but if it is not experienced on a level that brings healing to the childhood hurt and anger at not feeling unconditionally loved, a lifestyle of resentment is often the result. When that childhood frustration encounters the laws and rules of religion, an environment is created in which the older brother syndrome may flourish.

Before I received the life-changing revelation of the Father's love, I would be out on the road ministering, slaving for the Lord, for weeks at a time, and my resentment and frustration would often overflow onto my wife and family when I arrived home. Trisha knew she had better be on time to the airport to pick me up when my flight came in. If she was late, she had better have a good reason. Traffic was not a good enough excuse; she should have anticipated any potential problems and left earlier to compensate for the delays.

My demands were constant and unrelenting: Why haven't the kids cleaned their rooms? Haven't you taken the garbage out yet? Why aren't there clean sheets on the bed? To everyone outside of my family, I appeared to be a holy and righteous minister—a man of integrity—who was giving his life in service to the Lord, but to my wife and children I lacked grace and mercy. I was all wrapped up in getting my own needs met. As the older brother, I was more concerned with people's performance than I was with intimate relationships.

THE WAY HOME

How was I able to relinquish this attitude and lifestyle and experience a true homecoming to the Father's house? The transition from the love of the law to an embracing of the law of love required a repositioning of my heart and attitudes.

1. First of all, I came to an awareness of my sin. I noticed symptoms of the older brother syndrome in my life, and I realized I was in need of a homecoming with my Father.

2. I moved to a state of repentance. I needed a change of heart so deep that it reached to my core attitudes of self-love, resentment and envy. I saw how deeply I had hurt those around me with my legalism and demeaning tones. I began to understand how much it wounded my children when I valued my ministry over time spent with them. When my heart began to break because I felt the pain that I had caused, I was ready for the homecoming to the Father's house.

3. I asked for and received forgiveness from God for believing the lie about His nature that says I must work to gain His love and acceptance. I relinquished all of the anger, jealousy, criticism and judgmental attitudes to which I had clung so fiercely, and I allowed His Spirit to transform my very nature and character.

4. I needed to seek for forgiveness from those whom I had hurt. This is the principle of restitution— going to those to whom I had misrepresented the Father's love. When the revelation of God's love changed my heart, I realized the pain I had inflicted on those I love, and I set things right. When I relinquished the attitude of the older brother, being right no longer mattered as much as the restoration of the important relationships in my life.

5. Finally, in humility, I began to find my Father waiting with His arms outstretched to embrace me and to bring me back into His house of peace and rest.

Anticipate the homecoming your heavenly Father has planned for you. He understands your hidden core issues, your need for affirmation that may stem from your childhood. He sees the secret place in your heart that cries out for the unconditional love of a father, for the affirmation and affection that only He can provide. His compassion and mercy are available to you; He longs to bring you back into His house and for you to join in the celebration and the joy of the feast. He is not ashamed or angry at your misrepresentation of His love. He wants you in His loving embrace!

If you need this homecoming with your Father, pray this prayer and begin to return to the joy of your salvation:

> *Heavenly Father, I come before You with a repentant heart. I realize that I have been like an older brother in Your house, placing the love of the law above the law of love in my heart. I recognize that my attitude has been one of resentment, competition, striving and jealousy, and I see the damage this has caused to my relationship with You and my relationship with the people I love. I realize how much I require others to perform for my acceptance and love. I have sinned against love!*
>
> *Father, I turn from these attitudes and return to Your heart of love and compassion. Restore to me the joy of my salvation, when I was motivated by my love for You and my gratitude for Your sacrifice. I want to serve You with a pure heart, motivated by Your compassion and love for others. Thank You for welcoming me back into Your house and allowing me to join in the celebration. In Jesus' name, amen.*

QUESTIONS FOR DISCUSSION

1. Describe your initial salvation experience, when you first came to know God. In what ways was it similar to the experience of the rebellious son? Were there any older brothers who impeded your homecoming to the Father? Have you forgiven them?

2. What church disciplines, such as prayer, fasting or tithing, do you regularly practice? How do they promote or hinder your relationship with God or other Christians?

3. Do you ever find yourself comparing your ministry or service to God with that of other Christians? What is the result of this comparison?

4. Do you see any of the symptoms of the older brother syndrome in your attitudes toward your family, other Christians or your own ministry? What steps might you need to take to return to a heart of compassion for others?

Chapter Six

Dealing With Father Issues

"M y, what big ears you have!"
I have heard comments like this all of my life. I'm not sure what God was thinking when He created me, but as a child He had fitted me with some of the largest, Dumbo-sized ears anywhere.

Unfortunately, my ears were the same size when I was born as they are now, so while today my head has finally grown out enough to balance out their monstrosity, when I was growing up, it was a different story. I was teased mercilessly as a child, and until I was forty years old, I could hardly look in a mirror without feeling depressed.

When my youngest son was born, it was obvious from day one that he had inherited the worst of my physical traits, my gargantuan ears. If anyone ever saw our baby pictures side by side, all they could say was, "My goodness!"

When the day arrived for Joshua to start school, I sent him off, hoping for the best. But it was inevitable. As he got off the school bus at the end of the day, he was sobbing.

"Dad, the kids made fun of me all day long! Everybody laughed at my ears. I never want to go back to school again!"

My son was experiencing a wound, one that could potentially last a lifetime. It was a defining moment in his life, and I knew it. I immediately took him in my arms, held him tight and told him how handsome he was.

Then I went and took out my own baby pictures and showed him what I looked like when I was his age. We looked just like identical twins, and I asked him, "Who do you want to look like when you grow up, Joshua?"

He answered without hesitation, "I want to look just like you, Dad!"

"Then, son, you never have to worry about what anybody says again. You are your dad's beloved son, and I love you. You are going to be the most handsome man when you grow up. So when people laugh at you now, just remember that you're going to look just like your dad someday!"

That conversation changed my son's life. From that day on, whenever anyone laughed at his ears, he laughed right back and thought to himself, *That just means that someday I'm going to look exactly like Dad!*

My son never had to go through the suffering that I went through, because when I faced the taunts of other children, my own father never comforted or protected me. He was not able to express love, comfort or affirmation when I needed it the most, and as a result, I often experienced pain and rejection I should never have had to feel. Fortunately, a revelation of the Father's love for me helped to break the cycle of pain, and I was able to comfort Joshua when he needed it. Instead of carrying that wound throughout his life, the pain never entered his heart. But uncomforted pain can leave a wound for a lifetime.

No matter how well your earthly father may have provided for you, even if you lived in a large home, wore the nicest clothing and ate the best food, if you didn't feel protected, comforted or safe in his presence, you may never feel safe anywhere else in your life. If the wounds of your childhood were left uncomforted by your earthly father, you may never feel comforted in God's presence. And you may spend your entire life looking for a place of safety and belonging, longing for a home.

Unresolved father issues from childhood can often be a major cause of emotional pain later in adulthood. Adult pain is often wired to childhood pain. Many family counselors believe that the majority of a child's identity is formed through the father-child relationship. When that relationship becomes skewed, children may grow up with difficulties relating to other male authority figures later in life. And when they come to Christ and become born again, the issues that they have with their earthly fathers often transfer to the new relationship they have with their heavenly Father.

In the parable of the rebellious son that Jesus told in Luke 15, both of the sons had father issues. The younger son did not value his father for the intimate relationship he could have had with him; instead, he focused on what his father could do for him. For some reason, he felt the need to demand what he believed was his, and then he squandered it on an immoral lifestyle. The older brother also had a poor relationship with his father. Although he had lived in the father's house for years and was faithful to be a loyal and obedient son, he was no closer to the father's heart than his immoral brother was. He apparently had hidden resentment and conflict in his heart that prevented him from a close, intimate relationship with his father.

To whichever brother we can relate, whether we are running from God by living a life of sin and immorality or striving to please Him with our hyperreligious activity but not allowing Him to touch our heart, our relationship with God is highly influenced by the relationship we had with our earthly father. The father issues we have may be unconscious or conscious, but until they are resolved through an experiential revelation of the heavenly Father's love, we have difficulty experiencing the comforting, affectionate love that He has for us. Our anger, fear and distrust, which is often rooted in our hidden core pain, easily spills over into many areas of our lives—our marriages, our families, our careers, our ministries, our walk with God—and the effects can greatly hinder a life of intimacy and love.

FOUR BASIC EMOTIONAL NEEDS

Father issues can come in many different forms. Your father may have insulted you verbally, and his words, whether intentionally or unintentionally, may have echoed in your mind since your childhood. He may have made promises that were left unkept. Or he may have rejected or abandoned you, causing a deep grief that has never been healed.

All human beings have four basic emotional needs. As children, we look to our parents, and from three years of age and older we especially look to our fathers, to meet these needs for us. The family is the place where children learn how to relate to the world, and the lessons learned there are ones carried throughout a lifetime. When these four needs go unmet in childhood, it becomes very difficult for a person to develop healthy relationships with God or with other people later in adulthood.

1. The need for unconditional expressed love

It is not enough for a father to provide shelter, food and clothing for his children. It is not even enough for a father to have loving feelings for them. Those feelings must be communicated and expressed in a way that is meaningful to the child. Every child is different, and each one will experience love in a different way. One child may need extra time spent playing with him and his favorite toys; another will crave physical touch, hugs and kisses or being cuddled on daddy's lap. Fathers who spend the time to get to know their children will learn to express their love to them in the way that means the most.

2. The need to feel secure and comforted

Every child needs to feel safe, both physically and emotionally. A father can provide a secure environment by putting locks on the doors and keeping their children safe from the monsters in the closet. But children also need to know that their families and households are emotionally safe and that they always have a safe place in their father's heart, no matter how much they fail. Explosive anger and rage are frightening experiences for many children, and too often they become a reality. They need an atmosphere of unconditional love and acceptance so that their emotional well-being is secure.

3. The need for praise and affirmation

Even adults want other people to say good things about them. Children especially need this from their parents, and many sons and daughters spend their lives trying to gain the approval of their fathers. Dr. James Dobson has stated that it takes at least forty words of praise to counteract just one word of criticism in a child's heart. Many fathers have the best of intentions, and they try to be tough on their kids to help prepare them for the "real" world. But children will become better prepared for life when their self-esteem and value are recognized and encouraged by their fathers, more so than if they live under the shadow of constant criticism.

4. The need for a purpose in life

Fathers have a responsibility to cultivate their children's talents and gifts. Everyone needs to find a sense of value, a belief that their lives mean something and that they can make a difference. Children need to be told that they are special, that they have something unique to offer the world and that they are a gift of God's love to the world.

FATHER FLAWS: THE LENS THROUGH WHICH WE VIEW FATHER GOD

Children look to their fathers to meet these four emotional needs, but unfortunately, no earthly father is perfect. Even the best of us fail to meet all of our children's needs all of the time. At some point, disappointments, hurts and wounds will inevitably take place, and these may cause what I call "father flaws" to form in the hearts of our children. The leftover pain and wounds from childhood can create a lens through which adults later view the world and God.

Most earthly fathers will fall into one of six different categories, each of which creates a different home environment for the children. Many fathers will not completely fit into one certain category; they may have characteristics of more than one fathering style. As you read through each type of father, think back to your own childhood and try to determine how your earthly father related to you. Each type of father can create different father issues in the adult children and different hindrances to an intimate relationship with God. I am not trying to stir up old wounds, but help you identify where strongholds may be holding you back from intimacy and love. Ask the Holy Spirit to reveal to you any unresolved hidden issues you may still have with your own earthly father that may be affecting your ability to relate to your heavenly Father and to receive His affectionate love.

THE GOOD FATHER

When thinking back to their childhoods, many Christians would argue that they came from a "good home" with fathers who seemed to love them and provide for their needs. However, while there may be many good fathers in the world, there is no perfect earthly father, and it is difficult for any dad, no matter how good his intentions may be, to raise a child without creating any father issues whatsoever.

Good fathers are just that: good fathers. They provide for their children in many ways. Physically, the children have a solid roof over their heads, nice clothes to wear and good food to eat. Emotionally, these fathers are stable and loving, spending time with their children, meeting their needs for security and affirmation and seeming to do everything a father should. It would seem that children raised in such homes would grow up without any negative repercussions in their adult lives.

But the issues these children have as adults are often very subtle. Sometimes they are unable to let go of the stability of their relationship with their earthly dads sufficiently enough to develop a strong relationship with Father God. Some of these children may even become pastors or ministers because, having become overly attached to their earthly fathers, they may not develop an intimate relationship with God and can only find their adult identity in serving Him rather than being intimate with Him.

The bond between a good father and his child may become an unhealthy dependence later in life if the adult child continues to look to the father for his or her ultimate source for love and security. Some daughters may experience difficulty "leaving and cleaving" when the time comes for them to leave their father's home and become a wife to their husband. They may compare their spouse with the unattainable characteristics of their father, with the spouse rarely measuring up.

Other times, situations may arise that leave the father unable to keep a promise or meet every one of his child's needs. Even the most well-meaning good father cannot control every situation in his children's lives. This may end up being even more of a disappointment if the children have grown to have unrealistic expectations of their father.

My wife, Trisha, was raised in a "good home," and she had this type of father throughout her childhood. He worked hard to provide for his family, and he loved and cherished her like a princess. But circumstances occurred that were beyond his control. He was a truck driver for many years, but when Trisha was about twelve years old, he had a heart attack. At that point, his health began to decline, and he eventually was taken off the road. The family's finances suffered, and they sank from a middle-class income into poverty.

Trisha's father wanted so much to continue to provide all the things that his children had grown accustomed to, and he would continually talk about all the things he planned to buy or do for them once things got better: the Christmas presents he would buy, the vacations they would take. But year after year went by, and few of these promises were kept. To make matters worse, his health continued to decline, and despite all of the fervent prayers for healing made by their family, their pastor and their church, Trisha's father died when she was twenty years old.

Broken promises, disappointment and grief all opened the door for hidden lies in Trisha's heart, despite the good intentions that her father had had. These became issues in her heart that carried over into her adult life as a wife to me and a mother to our children. She found it difficult to trust in a God to whom she had prayed so desperately for her father's health, only to be so deeply disappointed when he died. She was constantly anxious over the state of our finances, because she feared experiencing again the poverty she had known in childhood. In her heart, she found it hard to believe any of the promises that I made to her because of so many broken promises her father had made, and it became an area of contention in our marriage. Until she was able to relinquish the pain, disappointment and despair that had been tied to her relationship with her dad, she could not experience the love and security of her heavenly Father deep within her heart. But in 1996, when she did have a deep and intimate encounter with Father's comforting love, it made all the difference, and she was able to move beyond her father issues into a joyous life of security, love and intimacy in most of her relationships.

THE PERFORMANCE-ORIENTED FATHER

Stringent demands for a child's perfect obedience and high performance standards, if not tempered with large amounts of expressed love, affirmation and praise, often result in many problems later in life. The performance-oriented father is very common in America today because, as a whole, our society rewards individuals who perform successfully, whether it be in sports, careers, academics or the financial market. This father often pro-claims that he loves you, but that love is only expressed when you have measured up to his rigid expectations.

Little Susie may work very hard to make good grades, and when it is time to take her report card home to her dad, she is so happy because she thinks he will be pleased with her. When she hands him the report card, he looks at it and begins to praise her, "Wonderful, Susie! Look at that A in math. I'm so proud of you! But wait…What's this? A C in geography? You should be doing better than that. What a disappointment!"

This attitude can carry over into the church, especially into the families of pastors and ministers. While we might think that pas-tors' kids should be the happiest, healthiest children on the block, in reality, they are often the ones who feel the greatest pressure to earn the love and affirmation of their parents and, ultimately, the approval of God. One survey revealed that 80 percent of adult children of pastors surveyed will experience some form of psychi-atric care for depression in their lives.[1] A primary root of depres-sion is performance-orientation. No one can ever do everything right all of the time because we are only human beings, and we all experience failure. But after twenty or thirty years of constantly striving for perfection, fear and depression begin to creep into the heart of this adult son or daughter. They may be born-again, Spirit-filled, new creations in Christ, but they still believe that God will only be pleased with them when they read the Bible enough or when they have prayed at least an hour a day. Eventually, if the pattern continues, they can collapse into spiritual burnout, unable to hear God's voice or sense His presence at all.

Boundaries and standards are good, and fathers should encour-age their children to be the best that they can be. But when expressed love and approval become tied to how well the child can perform, problems may result. Any criticism or demands for per-formance must be tempered with large amounts of affection and affirmation. My own father set impossibly high standards for me in sports; he wanted me to be the greatest tennis champion in the world. But if I didn't hit the ball right, he would not even smile. If I hit it into the net too many times, he would become angry, and the look on his face told me exactly what he thought of me: I thought that I was not good enough to have a place in his heart. I carried that pain from my childhood over to my relationship with God until I experienced a deep revelation of His unconditional love for me—that there was nothing I could do to earn His approval, but that He was simply pleased with me being His own beloved child.

THE PASSIVE FATHER

The passive father makes no great demands on his children, but neither is there any overt rejection. He simply fails to be home even when he is home. He is not able to demonstrate any sort of love or affection at all, usually not intentionally, but because he himself never received these things from his own father. This may even become a generational or a cultural stronghold that is passed down from father to son for centuries. European families generally show very little affection or tenderness; Asian fathers generally are shame based and have very high expectations of successful performance from their children. These generational strongholds must be broken before the familial traits can be changed.

Passive fathers don't speak the words of love that their children need to hear; they don't reach out to their sons and daughters with warmth, hugs or kisses or time cuddled on his lap. He may be physically present in the home, but he isn't able to allow himself to be known. He does not share his joys, his hopes, his sorrows or his disappointments with his wife or children. He does not experience life with his family; he simply lives his life under the same roof.

Many times these fathers are workaholics, or they may be military fathers. Both of these situations require a man to put his emotions on the back burner in order to survive on the job. But when these men come home to their wives and children, they have never learned to move their emotions forward to relate to their families in a loving and comforting way. Pastors sometimes also fall into this category; a minister often handles so many emotional situations throughout the day that when he comes home in the evening he is exhausted. He has spent so much of his emotional energy helping other people that there is nothing left for his own family.

When you have been raised in the home of a passive father, your relationship with God may be devoid of passion and joy. Discipline, form and duty keep things safe because you have become uncomfortable with any show of emotion. When relating to God, you often will have a mental or intellectual assent to the gospel, but you rarely let the Father touch your heart and truly taste of His love. You know God loves you, but from afar, distant and impersonal.

These are quite often the adults who are the quickest to criticize any "emotional" move of the Holy Spirit in the church. Any weeping or loud rejoicing or praise to the Father causes them to feel extreme discomfort. But walking in the Spirit should be an emotional encounter. It's all about love, joy and peace much more than it is about the study of doctrine or theory. God wants to touch our hearts and emotions; He wants to restore healthy emotions in our relationships. (See Galatians 5:22–23; 1 Corinthians 2:4, AMP.)

THE ABSENTEE FATHER

Today in America this father is becoming more and more common. The absentee father is the one who is no longer physically present in the home. This could have been caused by a number of reasons: death, divorce or abandonment. Fifty percent of children in America wake up each morning with someone other than their natural birth father in the home. If they are not living with their birth father, too often the father figure they are relating to does not have a strong interest in meeting the emotional needs of that child. There are exceptions, of course; there are those godly stepfathers who step in and love their stepchildren as if they were their own, but that is a rare occurrence.

Children who have had an absentee father may face abandonment issues, and it may be very difficult for them to relate to God. Even if they do foster a relationship with Him, there may be a sense of fear that at some point, He may not be there for them just as their earthly father wasn't. This can also result in striving to please God in order to appease an unconscious guilt they may feel for somehow being at fault for their father leaving. But the heavenly Father tells us, "I will never leave you nor forsake you" (Heb. 13:5, NKJV). These children need an experiential revelation of God's presence and unconditional love in their lives.

THE AUTHORITARIAN FATHER

Authoritarian fathers are those fathers who are more interested in the love of law than in the law of love. They go beyond the performance-oriented fathers and sternly demand immediate, unquestioned obedience from their children. There is no real emotional relationship that is fostered between the father and the child; the only emotions that seem to be present are intimidation and fear.

These fathers are usually very selfish; the entire life of the family must revolve around them and their needs. They do not recognize the unique individuality of each child; they may see them as pawns to be used for getting their own needs met.

Children raised in such homes often see God as the Great Cop in the sky, a harsh authoritarian figure to be feared and obeyed rather than a loving Father to be enjoyed and cherished. They may strive so hard to meet His requirements that they feel more like servants rather than children whom the Father loves.

The Abusive Father

Verbal, emotional, physical or sexual abuse is becoming more and more common in families throughout the United States. If you have been abused in any of these ways, you often need more than just counseling or psychological therapy to be free of the deep pain and anger; you may need deep healing that can only come through the Holy Spirit pouring the love of God into your heart (Rom. 5:5).

Abuse, especially sexual abuse, creates one of the deepest wounds a child can ever receive, for it often results in tremendous hidden core pain. It can violate the trust the child has placed in authority and can affect all of his relationships for the rest of his life. Sexual abuse can leave children consumed with hidden fears and a deep distrust of God, pastors, other authority figures and other men. It can create feelings of guilt and a profound sense of shame and unworthiness. It can leave children feeling as if they did something to deserve to be treated so badly. And underneath it all, there can be tremendous repressed anger, much of it focused on God for allowing the abuse to take place.

Read the following testimony of one beautiful young lady who has experienced the Father's love:

> I was sexually abused by my father at age seven during my parents' separation and divorce. According to counseling professionals, the recollection of my memory indicates it was probably repeated abuse, but my heart detached from my intellect to protect itself, so I have no way of knowing how often the abuse occurred. During that time, as a little girl, God touched my heart during Vacation Bible School; I knew I wanted to follow Him. I thought God could make the pain go away. I began a lifelong search for God's love.
>
> In the absence of a father figure and lack of spiritual rearing, I sought comfort from older men who only wanted to use me sexually. From the time I was thirteen until I was

twenty-one years old, I was willing to have sex with men to get the affection I never received from my dad. As I grew up, I knew this was wrong. I became involved in religious activity, but never really knew the Lord. (I thought Jesus was a religion.) I went from psychiatrist to psychiatrist, paying thousands of dollars to get emotionally healed. I was dependent on antidepressants just to survive.

I was radically saved in 1992 after going through a painful divorce. For the first time in my life I experienced the grace of God and was set free from depression. But soon, I struggled with sexual sin again and could not break the pattern of my past. I even earned my masters degree in rehabilitation counseling, yet it left me without insight to change the destructive patterns of my life. I had sought all of my adult life how to be free from sexual sin.

I heard about Shiloh Place Ministries and signed up for one of their retreats. Their staff ministered emotional healing and deliverance to me. I had experienced a lot of deliverance previously, but no one could get the wound healed, so the fear of falling into sin haunted me because I had a need to perform for men. I feared God, spiritual authority and all male authority figures. I thought if I could not walk in sexual purity, my only alternative was suicide. I gained intellectual understanding of how much God loved me, but it was not until I was in the prayer line at an SPM meeting, when Jack prayed over me and called out the ages when I had been sexually abused/used, that my understanding went beyond being intellectual. That night, God began to restore love to me and I began to trust Him. I could be alone with God, and I knew He would not abuse me. For the next year, I would get up every morning, only to find the Spirit of the Father waiting in my living room to fellowship with me and impart more of His love to me. Father took me through a daily walk of restoring love and innocence. He walked me through all the years of shame, and for the first time in my life, I felt clean. I knew God as my loving Daddy.

After that night in the prayer line, I returned to my job the next week. People came up to me and asked me what had changed. My life was transformed by the experience of the love of God, and from my initial encounter with Shiloh Place Ministries, I have been free from sexual sin.

I believe in counseling. I believe in prayer ministry and healing lines. These things can help prepare a heart for the breaking forth of the Father's affectionate love in our core area of need, an experience in the Father's embrace.

WHAT IS REQUIRED OF US FOR HEALING?

Listen, O daughter, give attention and incline your ear; forget your people and your father's house; then the King will desire your beauty; because He is your Lord, bow down to Him.

—PSALM 45:10–11

Father, forgive them; for they do not know what they are doing.

—LUKE 23:34

What is required of *you* for healing? To give your father a gift he may not deserve—forgiveness! You must be willing to forgive your earthly father for each area in his life where he failed to represent the Father's love. If you do not forgive, then you may end up carrying the baggage of father issues around for much of your life. You may end up getting your identity from the pain and disappointments of your earthly father's house. Hurt people hurt people! He gave you all that he had to give.

Seeking to place blame upon your father for the problems you are having in life may increase your troubles and the sense of separation you feel from God. You may have been innocent of the wounding you experienced in your father's house, but you are accountable for your dishonor (disrespect) toward your father.

"Honor your father and mother…that it may be well with you, and that you may live long on the earth" (Eph. 6:2–3). Healing begins when you begin to forgive, take personal responsibility for present relational issues and do not seek to blame others for them. (See chapter eight.)

Many people feel wounded by feeling that their fathers have never blessed them. I believe that Father God wants to impart to us the Father's blessing that we may have lacked, even as He blessed His Son at the Jordan River, saying, "Thou art My beloved son, in Thee I am well-pleased" (Mark 1:11). Father also wants to affirm us for being His children. "See how great a love the Father has bestowed upon us, that we should be called children of God; and such we are" (1 John 3:1).

When we release our earthly fathers and begin to come to the Father as a little child in need of a father's love, we will begin to receive increasing revelation of Father God's love that is more powerful than any father issues we have carried through life. He will not ignore your cry for a father. No longer do you have to surrender yourself to the wounds within your father's house, for Father God is calling you to come home to Him.

> For my father and my mother have forsaken me, but the LORD will take me up…A father of the fatherless…God makes a home for the lonely; He leads out the prisoners into prosperity…For in Thee the orphan finds mercy. I will heal their apostasy, I will love them freely.
>
> —PSALM 27:10; 68:5–6; HOSEA 14:3–4

> I will not leave you as orphans; I will come to you…He who has My commandments and keeps them, it is he who loves Me; and he who loves Me shall be loved by My Father, and I will love him, and will disclose Myself to him…If anyone loves Me, he will keep My word; and My Father will love him, and We will come to him, and make Our abode with him.
>
> —JOHN 14:18, 21, 23

For the Father Himself loves you, because you have loved Me, and have believed that I came forth from the Father.

—John 16:27

Sample Prayer for Release and Healing From Father Issues

Father God, I come to you in Jesus' name. Thank You that the door to Your house is always open to me and that I do not have to fear Your loving presence. You tell me in Psalm 45:10–11 to let go of my identity that is in my father's house so that I can enter into the fullness of Your love. I come to You for Your help so that I can release and forgive my father.

- Choose to forgive your father for each way he hurt and disappointed you. Be detailed in speaking specific words of forgiveness for each moment of wounding that comes to mind. This may take some time. It is helpful to have a prayer partner lead you.

- Ask God to show you any specific memory that still influences your thought life, attitudes or actions. Ask God to enter into that situation and bring comfort to the hurting child. Be still and quietly wait on God's love to touch that area. Let the verses about God's love and comfort come to mind in order to displace distracting thoughts.

- Lay your father at the foot of the cross and release him. Lay at the cross the pain, the anger, the bitterness and the disappointments. Now turn and walk away.

- Turn to Father God. *I have nowhere to go for love. I know the door to Your house is always open. You said that You would not leave me like an orphan. I ask You, Father, to come to me now and reveal Your love and Fatherhood for me. I choose to receive You as a Father to me. I choose to be Your child.*

- Begin to pray, or have someone pray over you, the scriptures about Father's love for you from chapter three, "You Are Father's Happy Thought."

- Put on music about Father's love for you; let the message penetrate your heart as you sit quietly meditating upon the Father's love. Spend some time daily doing this, and allow His love to comfort you. (Music can be obtained through Shiloh Place Ministries.)

There may be a need to seek professional counseling or healing prayer ministry. You may want to consult your pastor for recommendations.

QUESTIONS FOR DISCUSSION

1. Which of the four emotional needs were met in your childhood? Which do you feel were unmet? How are you seeking for Father God to meet these needs in your adulthood?

2. Father flaws, the negative experiences we had with our earthly fathers in childhood, can become lenses through which we view the world. What father flaws do you feel remain in your heart? How can they be changed?

3. There are six types of fathers listed in this chapter. Which of these best describes the relationship you had with your own father? (You may list more than one.)

4. What benefits, if any, did you receive from this type of relationship you had with your father? What negative consequences were there? How have these affected your adult relationships with God and with other people?

Chapter Seven

Dealing With Mother Issues

O ut of all of the creatures in the animal kingdom, storks are some of the most loving and tender. Mother storks watch over and carefully nurture their babies, and adult storks care for one another and meet each other's needs throughout all of life. Even when a stork becomes older and has difficulty keeping up with the others, another stork may fly alongside the elderly stork and allow it to rest its wings on theirs. These storks help each other to fly more effectively, and they are constantly touching, nurturing and protecting one another. It is no wonder that the Greeks used the word *storge* to describe family love. It is *storge* love that speaks of nurture, empathy, affection and tenderness.

Among humans, just as it is in the animal kingdom, mothers are the primary caregivers and dispensers of *storge* love in the child's first two years of life. The father's primary years of influence are the third through fifth year, but the mother is the one who carries the baby in her womb imparting warmth, security and trust. She then births the child, draws him to her breast, tenderly cares for him and nurtures him. One of the connotations of the word *nurture* is "to cause something to come forth." The mother's *storge* love imparts faith in the child to trust bonding, to receive love and to give love.

Your relationship with your mother was your first experience with love. Even in the womb, you either felt the emotional nurture and tenderness of your mother or you didn't, and those vital, tender bonding experiences helped form the way you felt about yourself, the world and God. During the nine months spent in the womb and throughout the first two years of life, the mother figure is the most important figure in a child's life, having the strongest influence by the way she nurtures and expresses love to the child.

David demonstrated this principle in Psalms when he declared to the Lord, "Yet Thou art He who didst bring me forth from the womb; Thou didst make me trust when upon my mother's breasts. Upon Thee was I cast from birth; Thou hast been my God from my mother's womb" (Ps. 22:9–10). Babies learn how to trust life, relationships and even God when they are held, cuddled, fed and nourished at their mother's breast. And without the mother's *storge* love, children may grow up with an inherent fear of relationships and life that may be difficult to uproot.

Storge love is demonstrated in three primary ways by mothers:

1. *Affectionate touch.* We were created for affection. Doctors have scientifically proven that without touch the body and the emotions become unhealthy. Touching someone says to them that they are important to you; they belong, and they have value. If we did not receive affectionate touch in the right way as a child, then in our teenage years we may allow ourselves to be touched in the wrong way.

2. *Eye contact.* The eyes are the windows of the soul where love is communicated to a child. They drink the love that flows to them from the eye contact with their parents. If children don't see understanding, loving looks in the eyes of their parents, it can leave a wound that remains unhealed all through life. They then may feel awkward, insecure, separate and out of place in their relationships.

3. *Tone of voice.* Babies learn to bond and trust when their parents look them in the eye and speak to them loving words in an encouraging, gentle, tender and empathizing voice. It continues all

through the formative years in the child. Loving tones nurture the soul and help children feel acceptance and value so they can walk free from the fear of rejection and failure.

Nurturing mothers who walk into a room in which there is a baby seem to temporarily lose their sanity. They start babbling in baby talk: "Goo, goo, ga, ga," they coo, often to the disbelief of their male counterparts. When a mother picks up a baby, her tone, her mannerisms and everything about her change; love and tenderness begin to flow through her to that child. She would do everything possible to meet the needs of that infant, and the baby can sense that through her body language. She is demonstrating *storge* love, and the child develops a godly belief that he or she will be comforted and that his or her needs will be met by others. In later years, they believe their needs will be met by God.

THE MOTHER HEART OF FATHER GOD

In the very nature of God, there is a mother's heart, the *storge* love that comforts us in tenderness and compassion. This has been present since the beginning of time, even in the creation of the world.

> Then God said, "Let Us make man in Our image, according to Our likeness; and let them rule over the fish of the sea and over the birds of the sky and over the cattle and over all the earth, and over every creeping thing that creeps on the earth." And God created man in His own image, in the image of God He created him; male and female He created them.
>
> —GENESIS 1:26–27

How could God have created the female "in His own image" if there is not some aspect to His nature and character that is feminine? While I am not taking it to the extent that a few religious leaders would by saying that God is actually female, the nature of God does encompass both masculinity and femininity. The masculine heart cries out to do, to form and create, to initiate, to know wisdom and to rationalize and intellectualize. The feminine heart seeks to be; it longs for communion and connection, to bond and to know and to be known emotionally. The power to receive lies in femininity; the power to give lies in masculinity. This principle is beautifully demonstrated in God's creation of the sexual union between husband and wife: The man gives his sperm, and the woman receives it.

Men, while predominantly masculine, have a feminine part to their natures, and to reject it they often reject compassion, empathy, nurture, comfort, intimacy and/or the ability to receive and give expressed love. In so doing, they can deny a portion of what God has created them to be, and thus they can easily give themselves over to finding their identity in performance, creating and doing. They may begin to devalue emotions and intimacy; they may value logic and being analytical and intellectual over tenderness, affection and warmth in relationships. Women likewise should not deny their masculine sides, or they may reject the analytical, intellectual aspects of their being.

The heart of both giving and receiving, of both action and relationship, is present in the nature of God who created the universe. He not only wants to produce miracles for His people, but He also wants to experience intimacy with them. He wants to provide His children with His love, but He wants to receive love from them as well. He created us for love and intimacy. God values femininity because He desires intimacy with us, and He has placed mothers on the earth to impart to their children, both boys and girls, how to cultivate intimate, compassionate, caring and loving relationships.

Throughout the ages, the world has valued masculinity over and above femininity. In almost every world religion, even in many circles of Christianity, females are devalued and even degraded in the face of patriarchal societies. Many religions place their women under heavy veils of oppression and even perpetuate acts of violence against them. One of the more shocking practices, known as female circumcision, occurs in some African cultures. Young girls are mutilated to keep them from being consumed by sexual passions later in life. In some Middle Eastern countries, women are often blamed and punished when their husbands commit acts of adultery.

Could there be some unholy scheme to destroy femininity on the earth? For six thousand years, Satan has had a special hatred for women. He has sought to destroy and devalue femininity in the hearts of mankind since the day in the Garden of Eden when the Lord God gave the woman (femininity—compassion, intimacy, communion, the ability to receive love) the power to defeat him. The woman was not cursed, but the curse imposed was upon Satan that the woman would bring great harm to Satan's kingdom. Satan now fears a person who walks in the intimacy that femininity brings forth; thus he seeks to wound us in our relationship with our mothers so that we reject femininity and a life of intimacy.

> And the LORD God said to the serpent, "Because you have done this, cursed are you more than all cattle, and more than every beast of the field; on your belly shall you go, and dust shall you eat all the days of your life; and I will put enmity between you and the woman, and between your seed and her seed; He shall bruise you on the head, and you shall bruise him on the heel."
>
> —GENESIS 3:14–15

Could it be that it is easier for the world to value masculinity because the enemy has sought to make the world and religion a performance-oriented society that values performance and productivity more than intimate, caring relationships? Could it be that the church has lost some of its authority and power to overcome the evil one by putting a higher value upon those who walk in masculine qualities (building and producing) than they do upon those who value qualities of femininity (communion and intimate, connected relationships)? Could it be that we need a healthier balance of both before we see a world revival?

THE MOTHER WOUND

Breaches in the mother's love, whether they are caused intentionally or unintentionally, can leave wounds in a child's heart that can last a lifetime.

My daughter, Sarah, was conceived during a very traumatic time for my wife and me. Our first child had already been born, but within a few months of his birth, he began having seizures that often caused him to stop breathing and forced my wife to rush him to the emergency room almost at the point of death. My wife was the one who did this because at that time, I was on a fishing boat twenty days or more out of each month. Trisha was left at home with a very sick child, with no way to contact her husband and with very little sources of comfort in her life. Storms would blow through—nor'easters with winds up to fifty to sixty miles per hour at sea—and she would know that I was out in twenty- to thirty-foot seas. She became consumed with fear, both for me and for our child, and as the situation wore on, she grew closer and closer to an emotional collapse.

Trisha's dream had always been to have a daughter, a little girl to play with, dress up and on whom to dote all of her motherly affections. But when the doctor told her that she was pregnant with our second child, she nearly came unglued.

"I can't be pregnant! I can't survive emotionally with what I am already going through—how will I be able to handle another baby?"

When I arrived home from sea and she told me the news, I was thrilled. Another baby! I couldn't wait to have another child, and I couldn't understand Trisha's despair.

"I don't want another baby right now! I can't handle it with you rarely home to help me!" She cried for three straight weeks.

For nine months, Trisha carried that child, Sarah, in her womb, and her attitude rarely changed. It has been proven that the thoughts and emotions of the mother will affect a child in her womb—that what the mother thinks, experiences and feels can influence the emotions of the baby inside of her.[1] At the moment of conception, a living spirit is created, and there is spirit-to-spirit communication between the mother and child in the womb. Just one thought can create a response in the child in the womb. A mother who has been addicted to cigarettes need only think about smoking, and the heartbeat of the baby will begin to rise. Studies reveals how children in the womb are affected by the environments of their mothers, and when Trisha was carrying Sarah, the little girl of her dreams, Sarah experienced all of the negative emotions that Trisha was experiencing. Without ever hearing the words verbally, could Sarah have begun to receive the message, "You are not welcome at this time of crisis in my life. You are not being called to life"?

After nine months of experiencing her mother's emotional crisis, it was finally time for Sarah to come into the world. It was a very difficult delivery. After over twenty hours of excruciating labor, Sarah had to be delivered by an emergency cesarean section, a traumatic event for both mother and child.

After the birth, Trisha went into a deep postnatal depression that lasted about a year. Throughout that time, the problems only increased with my continual absence, our son's illness and a newborn baby to take care of. Did Trisha love our daughter? Of course! She would have given up her own life for Sarah. But the emotional repercussions of those difficult times had seeded an ungodly belief in Sarah—a stronghold in her mind, will and emotions.

By the age of two, Sarah would beat up any four-year-old she could find. Essentially she did not "get along well with others." As she grew older, she rejected all forms of affection, was antisocial and was defiant of her parents or anyone who tried to tell her what to do. Although she performed well in school, receiving straight As most of the time, her attitude toward relationships and authority left something to be desired. Sarah was also a tomboy; she never had girlfriends in grade school, but she could whip most of the boys in any sport. She denied her femininity (bonding) and embraced only masculinity (performing). She had not allowed her femininity to be nurtured when she perceived rejection coming from her mother. Thus she rejected bonding to her mother's love, even after Trisha was healed of depression and sought to do everything to make up for the *storge* love that was missing during those months of crisis.

When Sarah was nine years old, we began learning many principles of healing for wounded hearts, and Trisha and I ministered healing prayer to those wounded places in Sarah's heart that hadn't felt received by her mother. With the mothering touch of God's love, we watched a tomboy begin to transform into our beautiful daughter, feminine and soft. She began to wear dresses, experiment with makeup and fix her hair; now, at twenty-one years of age, her beauty is difficult to surpass. She is still self-motivated, always excelling in whatever she puts her hand to, but now she is also in touch with her womanhood and is warm and affectionate. It is a beautiful thing to watch her femininity flourish. As a result, her relationships with her mom, others and myself have become so much healthier.

Sarah needed the expressed *storge* love of both her mother and father to learn how to balance her masculine and feminine sides. The mother's expressed love is so important to a child's development and ability to maintain healthy relationships with others, God and ourselves. So many people, even born-again, well-meaning, mature, Spirit-filled Christians, can be handicapped in the area of love and intimacy because they never learned to trust during the first two years of life and while on their mother's breast.

God created you for love! The family in which you grew up was not the family that God planned for you to have. God's plan was that Adam and Eve would have never sinned and that your whole life you would have experienced perfect love. Your mother and father were meant to express to you unconditionally affectionate love and to be a reflection of Father God's love for you. God's desire for you was that your childhood would be filled with love, acceptance, security, warmth and comfort—that you would learn to trust on your mother's breast, that you would be the apple of your father's eye, that there would never be one moment of pain, violation, discomfort or grief. He created you to be comfortable with loving, intimate relationships.

HEALING FOR THE MOTHER WOUND

Recently, after hearing me speak on being created for love, a couple came forward to the altar for prayer with their two small sons. They both fell to their knees broken and weeping. With a heart filled with exasperation over never feeling loved, the mother cried out, "I don't know how to love! I've never experienced the kind of love you spoke of!" Then her little boy, about five years old, ran up and held his mother in his arms. With a heart full of innocence, love and compassion he tenderly said, "Mommy, I'll show you how to love!"

Most of my adult life I shared the agony and frustration that this mother felt. I had feelings of love locked up inside of me, but love only seemed to come out reserved, with impatience or insensitivity. I felt inadequate to express love, so I showed love by the things I did more than by who I was to my family (masculinity absent of embracing femininity). This just left me and them frustrated and empty inside.

We men tend to get a little frustrated when we are asked to do something we don't know how to do. All this leaves our families without a sense of love, comfort, value and security. So we comfort ourselves (even as Christians) in our performance, addictions, compulsions, anger, isolation, insecurity and fears of failure and rejection.

Seeing the pain in my family, I sought out every book I could so that I might learn how to love my family more and be intimate with them. The more knowledge I accumulated, the more frustrated I became. Now I knew how to do it right, but it most often came out wrong. "What is the matter with me? I can't seem to do anything right at home, so why should I even try any more? I'll just busy myself ministering to others. At least that brings me a feeling of acceptance and value when I seem to fail so much at home!"

I had filled my mind with knowledge, but years ago I had closed down a part of my heart to love! As a small boy, my parent's marriage began to fall apart. The early years were good, but then everything seemed to start going wrong. At about twelve years of age, I closed my heart and rebelled against love and being a son. Something began to die inside of me. Because I was created for relationship, when I cut myself off from bonding in a healthy way, I was willing to bond to anything in an unhealthy way. We must experience love daily to be emotionally healthy! So many Christians are emotionally unhealthy because they have not received the right kind of love—*storge* love.

Storge is foundational to feeling secure and comforted. It quiets and brings rest to your soul and gives you vision and purpose in life. It makes you feel valued and gives you a sense that you belong. You begin to believe in yourself and develop faith to live and overcome. It equips you to conquer the fear of relationships and lowers walls of self-protection.

Because of the pain my parents were experiencing with the breakup of their marriage and my rebelling against being a son, I cut myself off from receiving this kind of love. I began to develop a heart of stone. "I'll let no one touch my deepest needs! I'll be self-reliant and independent of needing people!" This left my need for *storge* love unmet. God created me for this kind of love, and when I shut myself down from receiving it, all my *eros* (Greek word for physical attraction) love needs went haywire in my teen and early adult years. Unhealthy sexual desires and urges began to drive me in most of my relationships. Love to me seemed to have a sexual meaning only, so many of my thoughts toward women were erotic in nature. I tried getting my love needs met through *eros* instead of *storge*. It then carried over into most of my marital and family life, even as a Christian ministering emotional healing to many others. The ability for me to walk in pure, loving relationships was confined behind walls of fear and separation.

Then, in March 1996, I attended a Father Loves You Conference. One of the prayer ministers, a mature mother figure named Shirley Smith, ministered to me over my inability to receive or communicate *storge* love and the lack of comfort in my youth. She led the little boy within me in one prayer after another of repentance for each situation where I rebelled against being a son and against receiving love. For almost two hours I lay on the floor in her arms weeping. Hidden core pain from the heart of the little boy began to surface. It was agonizing for me to submit to love and to have the walls of fear, separation and isolation broken off of my emotions and habit patterns of thought.

For weeks following that experience, it was as if I had been born all over again. It was as if the innocence and meekness of a little child were being restored to my emotions. My family saw an immediate change in my personality. I went from being serious and reserved to being sensitive, comforting and soft. I even found it easier to laugh and play with my children, which had been unnatural in the past. I began looking for every opportunity to give *storge* love away to my family. At first, they were suspicious. They wanted to see if they could trust me, if this was real and would last.

Years later I'm still naturally expressing *storge*, and major walls have come down in our relationships. Before, I had tried to learn how to love, but love can never flow by the letter. There is no love in law! Love must flow from our spirit. When I confronted the hidden core pain and repented for rebelling against love and being a son, I was then able to submit to and receive the heavenly Father's love. Then I could humble myself to my family and be the gift of love to them that God created me to be!

The little boy at the altar repeated once more to his mother, "Mommy, I'll show you how to love!" Mom and dad broke, repenting to God for rebelling against intimacy and love and being a son and daughter in their youth. They then asked their sons to forgive them for not expressing *storge* love to them. Later, the husband and wife repented and ministered to one another. On the last night of the meetings the husband came to me and said, "My wife's face now has the look of an angel. I've never seen her more beautiful and radiant in my life. We both have embraced the truth that we are created for love, and it now is naturally flowing in our family one to another. We truly are becoming God's gift of love to each other and to our children!"

It is difficult to teach someone how to love until they have experienced it. Love and intimacy have been programmed into your genetic code because "His [God's] seed abides in him [you]" (1 John 3:9). The Greek word for *seed* is *sperma*. In Christ, God has placed His DNA, His genetic code within you, and God is love! You are created in His image! You cannot help but be conformed to the attributes of God's love! To fight against that, you will need drugs! You will need pornography! Or you will need a position, job or ministry where you can try to get your need for love and acceptance met. Why not yield now to being conformed to the image of God's love? Everything God has created within you has naturally been created for intimate, loving relationships. As you submit to love, it will become perfectly natural for you to do what your Father created you to do: to be an expression of His *storge* love to your family and then to the world!

GOD WANTS TO COMFORT YOU IN HIS LOVE

Even if you were physically or emotionally wounded as a child, you must not take on a victim mentality and believe that you are not responsible for any of your problems. You are the one who made the choice to turn to counterfeit affections to escape the pain or to turn to the mother heart of Father God for comfort and nurture and to experience His healing love. He longs for you to choose His love and to turn to Him no matter how much you have failed in the past. He loves you just the way you are; you do not have to do anything to experience His love for you. Does a little baby have to do anything to be loved? No! They must only choose to receive it!

Perhaps you need God's comfort or to experience His nurturing, mother love. Perhaps you never received *storge* love from your earthly mother, and the deep longing that has been left in your heart has caused you to turn to counterfeit affections to fill the void. Your mother may have forgotten or abandoned you, but God never has. No matter what type of mother you may have had, no matter how deeply she may have hurt or wounded you, God's unconditional love will always remember you, for you are written on the palms of His hands for all eternity.

> Can a woman forget her nursing child, and have no compassion on the son of her womb? Even these may forget, but I will not forget you. Behold, I have inscribed you on the palms of My hands.
>
> —Isaiah 49:15–16

See the mother heart of Father God waiting for you with outstretched arms to pull you upon His breast and to tenderly shower you with the affectionate love that you have longed for. Experience Him taking you upon His knee and comforting you with His loving arms.

> "That you may nurse and be satisfied with her comforting breasts, that you may suck and be delighted with her bountiful bosom." For thus says the Lord, "Behold, I extend peace to her like a river, and the glory of the nations like an overflowing stream; and you shall be nursed, you shall be carried on the hip and fondled on the knees. As one whom his mother comforts, so I will comfort you; and you shall be comforted in Jerusalem."
>
> —Isaiah 66:11–13

God knew you before you were ever conceived in your mother's womb. He loved you then, and He loves you now. There has never been a moment in time that He has not been reaching out to you and desiring for you to experience His affectionate love.

> I have loved you with an everlasting love; therefore I have drawn you with lovingkindness…Before I formed you in the womb I knew you, and before you were born I consecrated you.
>
> —JEREMIAH 31:3; 1:5

You have never been alone. You are not an accident. Father God created you and formed you in your mother's womb. He was there at the moment of your birth, ready to draw you into His arms. His thoughts toward you are filled with pleasure.

> For Thou didst form my inward parts; Thou didst weave me in my mother's womb…How precious also are Thy thoughts to me, O God! How vast is the sum of them! If I should count them, they would outnumber the sand…By Thee I have been sustained from my birth; Thou art He who took me from my mother's womb; my praise is continually of Thee.
>
> —PSALM 139:13, 17–18; 71:6

> Yet Thou art He who didst bring me forth from the womb; Thou didst make me trust when upon my mother's breasts. Upon Thee I was cast from birth; Thou hast been my God from my mother's womb.
>
> —PSALM 22:9–10

Although you may feel as though you have been emotionally rejected, abandoned or orphaned by your parents, God does not want to leave you in this condition. Even if you feel too wounded to come to Him, then He will come to you and not leave you like an orphan.

> For my father and my mother have forsaken me, but the

LORD will take me up…A father of the fatherless…God makes a home for the lonely…I will not leave you as orphans; I will come to you.

—PSALM 27:10; 68:5–6; JOHN 14:18

Say this aloud:

Mom,

I needed your comfort and expressed love so much. I didn't realize just how much I needed it until now. But Mom, because of your own emotional crisis, you weren't always able to give me the love that I needed. There were times when I needed to hear tender tones in your voice, but instead your words pierced my heart. There were times I needed to see in your eyes that you loved me, even when I failed in your eyes. There were times I needed to be drawn to the comfort of your breast and be held to your bosom, but you weren't there.

Mom, I forgive you for all of these times because you did not know what you were doing. You too were hurt and wounded in your youth. I forgive you for not knowing how to express love to me in the way that I needed. I forgive you for not knowing how to take me in your arms and provide that place of safety and comfort. I forgive your inability to open your heart to me in a way that would cause me to believe and trust fully in your love. I forgive you for your inability to provide me with the affectionate touch, the loving eye contact and the nurture in your bosom that I so needed.

I release you from any resentment or bitterness, and I speak the blessing of God over you. I honor you as my mother, the woman who gave me life and brought me into this world. Thank you for this gift of life. I commit myself to walk in an attitude of love and forgiveness toward you from this day forward.

God wants to make known His affectionate love to you, especially in the areas where you need His love the most. He declares that He will demonstrate His love to you, through one or more of your five senses, in a supernatural encounter with His *storge* love. He desires for you to be at home in His love.

> He who has My commandments and keeps them, he it is who loves Me; and he who loves Me shall be loved by My Father, and I will love him, and will disclose Myself to him…If anyone loves Me, he will keep My word; and My Father will love him, and We will come to him, and make Our abode with him…For the Father Himself loves you.
>
> —JOHN 14:21, 23; 16:27

Pray aloud:

> *Father God,*
>
> *I come to You longing to experience Your comforting heart, Your mothering heart. You are the only One who can meet the deepest need for* storge *love in my life.*
>
> *I bring my earthly mother to the foot of the cross and release her from any wounds and pain she caused in my life. Please forgive me for any resentment or bitterness I may have harbored toward her, and help me to walk in forgiveness and love toward my earthly parents.*
>
> *I confess that I have turned to counterfeit affections rather than to You to seek the* storge *love that I needed to fill the void in my heart. Some of the choices that I have made have been wrong, and I repent from any impure thoughts, fantasies or lust that I have allowed to breed in my mind and my emotions. Forgive me for not trusting You to meet all of my needs.*
>
> *I come to You now, lay my head on Your breast and rest peacefully, knowing that You love and care for me. In Jesus' name, amen.*

Now enter into the rest that you have been searching for all of your life. Find a quiet place to sit, and let gentle, loving music play over you. Enter into Father God's mother heart as He gives you the things that your own mother was not able to give. Receive a mother's affirmation and acceptance pouring into you. Receive nurture and comfort. Receive Him playing all the games with you that your mother was not able to play. Receive Him taking all the seriousness out and pouring in playfulness and joy and displacing the intensity. Receive Him drawing you into a special place in His heart where you will never be forsaken or forgotten. Enter into His rest as His affectionate love casts out all fear.

> Surely I have composed and quieted my soul; like a weaned child rests against his mother, my soul is like a weaned child within me.
>
> —Psalm 131:2

> There is no fear in love; but perfect love casts out fear…We love, because He first loved us.
>
> —1 John 4:18–19

> Blessed be the God and Father of our Lord Jesus Christ, the Father of mercies and God of all comfort; who comforts us in all our affliction so that we may be able to comfort those who are in any affliction with the comfort with which we ourselves are comforted by God.
>
> —2 Corinthians 1:3–4

> My child, you have always been with me, and all that is mine is yours…I will never desert you, nor will I ever forsake you.
>
> —Luke 15:31; Hebrews 13:5

QUESTIONS FOR DISCUSSION

1. Many people have difficulty experiencing the tender, nurturing side of God. Has this ever been a problem for you? Why or why not?

2. How has the relationship you had with your mother as a child affected any of your relationships today?

3. Are you comfortable with tenderness, affection and warmth?

4. Are you able to empathize with others' pain and seek to meet others' needs when they are hurting?

5. Describe an experience you may have had with the *storge* love of God. In what ways was it similar or dissimilar to the relationship you had with your mother?

Chapter Eight

Would You Rather Be Right or Have a Relationship?

N ot long ago I was asked, "What three people have helped most to mature you and to release you in ministry?" At first I thought it was those people in my life who have stood beside me and loved me through every trial and storm. But then I thought of several people who had not appeared to be loyal to me, those who sowed evil reports against me, those who tried to make themselves look good by exposing my faults and weaknesses to others, resulting in damage to my reputation and ministry.

I began to realize it is also some of the most hurtful, difficult relationships that have had some of the most dramatic impact for maturity and spiritual growth in my life. Without them, I may never have discovered some of the attitudes of pride, vindication, self-justification and self-righteousness that I was full of. They helped me see how opinionated I was and how important it was for me to be right all the time in order to prove my self-worth! For years, for me to admit fault meant that I must be broken and deserving of rejection or punishment. Unknowingly, it was some of the more hurtful relationships that helped lead me into a deeper revelation of the Father's embrace.

How many times have you valued being right over maintaining an intimate relationship with someone else and with God? How important has it been for you to have the last word? When you talk with your spouse or others, are you able to sit back and listen to what they have to say without constantly interjecting your own opinions? Are you afraid to show any weakness or vulnerability to your children? Do you always portray yourself as the strong, but firm, authority who is always right?

The need to be right often creeps into our relationships in subtle ways. Because self-love is something that every one of us as human beings struggle with at some point in our lives, we have felt the need to prove ourselves better than someone else.

The core issue is usually insecurity and fear that is rooted in a love deficit. When insecurity is combined with a love of law, it can breed hypocrisy and a self-righteous attitude, the opposite of the Spirit of Christ, which is a meek and humble heart. It is meekness (no self-assertion) that enables us to enter into His rest and prepares our heart to experience the Father's embrace. (See Matthew 5:5–11; 11:28–29.)

LIVING FOR LAW
OR LIVING FOR LOVE

As Christians it becomes very easy to value the letter of the law more than grace and mercy. It's funny how, in God's Word, He often turns what seems right and fair upside down. That is because Satan, who is a legalist, demands what is right and fair. He demands payment for our sins and is constantly pronouncing us "guilty, guilty, guilty." But it is God who does not want to give us what we deserve. He wants to give us an undeserved, unmerited gift. Satan traffics in law and in what is right and fair, what we deserve. God traffics in grace and mercy, what we do not deserve. Grace is a higher place than what is right and fair, and Satan can never operate in grace, only in accusations. (See Law and Grace chart on pages 131–132.)

Satan is the accuser of the brethren. (See Revelation 12:10.) His thoughts are always negative, accusatory, pointing out others' faults, blaming others, devaluing, dishonoring and demanding of rights and justice. Resentment, bitterness and a heavy heart follow Satan's thoughts.

LAW	Luke 6:35–38	GRACE
What is right and fair		An undeserved gift
Satan traffics in law		God traffics in grace
Satan is the prosecutor		Jesus is our Advocate
Satan is negative		God is positive
The accuser of the brethren		The Holy Spirit, the Comforter
The accuser accuses		The Comforter comforts

If you sow judgment…	Gal. 6:7–8	*If you sow grace…*
Eph. 4:26–27; Gal. 5:19–21		Eph. 4:29–31; Gal. 5:22–23
Accusatory thoughts & words		Edifying thoughts & words
Criticism		Encouragement
Fault-finding/blaming others		Seeing own fault first
Demands rights		Yields rights
Demands justice		Pronounces innocence
Rehearses wounds		Releases wounds
Unforgiveness and bitterness		Forgiveness and love
Rejects and devalues others		Accepts and values others

…you reap the law and release a self-imposed curse		*…you reap grace and release God's blessing*
Ps. 109:17–19, 29; Matt. 5:22		1 Pet. 3:9–13; Matt. 5:11–12
Resentment and bitterness		Innocence restored
Hardness and anger		Gentleness and meekness
Walls—heart of stone		Transparency/openness
Unforgiving relationships		Forgiving relationships

Pride	Humility
Bondage	Liberty
Anxiety, stress-related disease	Rest, peace, divine health
Wounded life	Healing, wholeness
There is no love in law ROM. 7:5	*Mercy triumphs* *over judgment* James 2:13

God is love; He is the opposite of Satan. God's thoughts are positive, comforting, edifying, encouraging, accepting, valuing and loving. Love "thinks no evil" (1 Cor. 13:5, NKJV). Grace, forgiveness and innocence follow after His thoughts. "For I know the thoughts that I think toward you, says the LORD, thoughts of peace and not of evil" (Jer. 29:11, NKJV).

Before I had this revelation, not knowing these truths brought much harm to my own life, family and ministry. It hindered me from finding rest in the Father's healing love. I would see others' wrongs or receive hurt from people, and my response would be for justice and what was right and fair (for me). I acted more like God's policeman and would begin to develop accusatory thoughts or words about those who I perceived had disappointed or hurt me. Then I would become negative, critical and devaluing toward them in my thought life. I did not realize it, but my own thoughts were coming into agreement with Satan's thoughts; I entered into judgment, and it hindered me from receiving healing and the blessings of God in my life.

After all, when people mistreat and disappoint us, it is only natural to feel hurt and wounded. But do we respond with God's grace? "Father, forgive them, for they know not what they are doing! They are only acting out of their own hidden core pain and rejection! Help me to cover them and restore relationship!" Or do we demand vindication, trying to justify and clear ourselves from blame? Do we try to make ourselves look good and innocent by exposing and talking about others' faults and thus making them look bad or in error?

Vindication can be one of the hungriest, most destructive appetites we possess. *Vindication is rooted in demanding our rights and justice for the wrongs done to us!* But God says, "Vengeance is Mine." It is His right, and it will cost us dearly to try helping Him out. When we do, God backs away from the situation and lets us handle things in our own fleshly, accusatory ways. Unknowingly, we are actually coming into agreement with Satan and hindering ourselves from experiencing the intimacy of the Father's embrace. When we decide we had better do something to help God straighten others out, we are definitely in need of God helping us!

BLESSING OR CURSE

We make the decision whether to receive mistreatment at the hands of others as a blessing or as a curse. God has promised a blessing if we respond with forgiveness and grace. But when we respond with accusation, vindication, faultfinding or blame shifting, we then give Satan a key to our front door; he can then come and go as he pleases in our house.

> Be angry, and yet do not sin; do not let the sun go down on your anger, and do not give the devil an opportunity.
>
> —EPHESIANS 4:26–27

A study by Christian educator Mark Virkler reveals that 80 percent of most Christian's thoughts are negative. "They didn't value me! They didn't speak to me! They were not concerned with my need! They! They! They!" You can take most of your thoughts or conversations about a difficult person in your life, and in one way or another line them up under one of two categories: thoughts of restoration and relationship, or thoughts of vindication and exposure. One way leads to blessing; the other way releases a self-imposed curse. Satan wants us to inherit a curse. If the majority of our thoughts and conversations are in agreement with him, he has a right to release the curse. When we place judgment on other people, we receive judgment in return. The psalmist David put it so well:

> He also loved cursing, so it came to him;
> And he did not delight in blessing, so it was far from him.
> But he clothed himself with cursing as with his garment,
> And it entered into his body like water,
> And like oil into his bones.
>
> —PSALM 109:17–18

God wants us to inherit a blessing. All we have to do is give the difficult person a gift that they may not deserve, a gift of forgiveness and grace.

> To sum up, let all be harmonious, sympathetic, brotherly, kindhearted, and humble in spirit; not returning evil for evil, or insult for insult, but giving a blessing instead; for you were called for the very purpose that you might inherit a blessing.
>
> —1 PETER 3:8–9

It really comes down to whether we would rather be right or have relationship. How often our thoughts come into agreement with Satan when we strive to be right in our relationships, especially at home. The biggest problem is, we usually are right about others' faults! But you can be right and have the wrong attitude, and you are dead wrong. Jesus didn't come to judge and accuse us, Satan did (John 3:17; 12:47; Rev. 12:10). Jesus didn't "grasp" for position or authority (Phil. 2:5–8); Satan did. Jesus sought to humble Himself. Satan sought to exalt himself (Isa. 14:12–14). Satan lost his position in God's presence. Christ was exalted to the right hand of the Father. When you choose the behavior, you choose the consequences! (See Law and Grace chart, pages 131–132.)

WIN A FRIEND AND INHERIT THE BLESSING

But I say to you who hear, love your enemies, do good to those who hate you, bless those who curse you, pray for those who mistreat you. Whoever hits you on the cheek, offer him the other also; and whoever takes away your coat, do not withhold your shirt from him either. Give to everyone who asks of you, and whoever takes away what is yours, do not demand it back. And just as you want men to treat you, treat them in the same way. And if you love those who love you, what credit is that to you? For even sinners love those who love them. And if you do good to those who do good to you, what credit is that to you? For even sinners do the same. And if you lend to those from whom you expect to receive, what credit is that to you? Even sinners lend to sinners, in order to receive back the same amount. But love your enemies, and do good, and lend, expecting nothing in return; and your reward will be great, and you will be sons of the Most High; for He Himself is kind to ungrateful and evil men.

—LUKE 6:27–35

These verses imply that there is no blessing or reward when we do good to good people. Blessing comes when we do good to the people who hurt us. The blessing is sonship—being placed in the Father's presence! We feel the full acceptance and unconditional love of the Father. We begin walking in a deeper intimacy with God and start taking on His spirit of grace, which releases intimacy in many of our relationships. We then start becoming more comfortable with love and forgiveness. This is the place where healing and the blessings of God begin to overtake you.

What is the best way to win over an enemy and enter into the blessing of the Father's embrace? In the above passage, Jesus revealed the path of blessing and intimacy:

- "Love your enemies," and you take on the spirit of Christ!

- "Do good to those who hate you," and you may make them your friend!

- "Bless those who curse you," and you inherit a blessing!

- "Pray for those who mistreat you," and you begin to see them through the loving eyes of the Father!

- "Love your enemies and do good," and you become like your Father and enter more deeply into His presence.

Jesus walked out these principles with the one who hurt Him most, Judas. He knew what was in Judas' heart from the beginning, yet Jesus continued to serve and minister to him for three years. He allowed Judas to minister beside Him. He washed Judas's feet right before the betrayal. He broke bread with him and lived faithful to the covenant of loyalty with Judas in spite of his actions toward Him. He never stopped receiving and valuing Judas. Where would we be if Jesus had not received Judas as a blessing and as the one who would move Him toward the cross?

Jesus' whole life demonstrated how we are to relate to other people. When He was mistreated and rejected, even when He was spat upon or when people attempted to kill Him, He responded with an attitude of grace and love. His modeling sets the standard for us to live by in our relationships with other people. Even with those people who are the most difficult to get along with, those who have hurt or rejected us, Jesus asks us to respond to them with the mercy that God has for us because He wants us blessed. "Be merciful, just as your Father is merciful" (Luke 6:36).

The law of love is a higher way than the love of law. Have you received the difficult people whom God has placed in your life as an instrument of blessing? If you do not value, honor and respect them, then you may be treating them like a curse, thus inheriting a curse! When we receive them as a blessing to help us find out what we are full of, then God can take every negative relationship and use it to bring us into spiritual maturity. This releases us to experience His love and then to be an instrument of His love to our family and to the nations!

> And as for you, you meant evil against me, but God meant it for good in order to bring about this present result, to preserve many people alive.
>
> —GENESIS 50:20

WHAT YOU GIVE IS WHAT YOU WILL RECEIVE

It helps me to look at it this way: It is not a matter of what I want to give to someone who hurts me. It is a matter of what I want to receive in the future from other relationships. Do I want to receive a hardened, wounded heart that separates me from intimacy with God and leads me into resentments, pride and walls of self-protection? Or do I want to enter into God's rest and walk in the joy of a lifestyle of forgiveness that produces a meek and gentle spirit? When I choose my response to wounding situations, I also choose what I will receive in the future from others.

> And do not judge and you will not be judged; and do not condemn, and you will not be condemned; pardon, and you will be pardoned. Give, and it will be given to you; good measure, pressed down, shaken together, running over, they will pour into your lap. For by your standard of measure it will be measured to you in return.
>
> —LUKE 6:37–38

The Bible is full of warnings that the standard by which we judge others will be the standard by which we ourselves will be judged. When I lived by the love of law, I had no revelation of the Father's love; thus all of my favorite scriptures were about judgment, righteousness, holiness and discipline. I breezed right past those on grace and mercy. My preaching and fathering had an angry edge to it. Because I felt I had to be perfect to measure up to God's standards, then that was the performance I required from others for me to accept them.

After a year or two in ministry, I began to see all the things wrong with the worldwide church and its leaders. I did not outwardly criticize or talk against leaders, except at home with my wife. On the inside there was the heart attitude of judgment against those who did not act like me, think like me, talk like me, have the same passion and vision in ministry as I did. It wasn't spoken outwardly, just an inward attitude that Christian leaders have missed it. So Trisha and I established Shiloh Place Ministries in 1991 in order to straighten out the lives of Christian leaders. But my heart attitude was wrong. I was not walking in love, but law; not grace, but judgment. What you give is what you will get!

I developed into a person who valued being right over relationship. I began valuing the people who seemed to have the same spirit as me and who promoted my ministry. But when I was around those who did not promote my ministry or me, I just did not feel comfortable around them—and they certainly did not seem comfortable around me. Please understand that all during these years I was a man of integrity and truth, the person teaching seminars on bitterness, forgiveness, marriage enrichment and healing the wounded heart. You do not know what you are in bondage to until you are free from it.

Outwardly, I had a smile on my face and honored other Christian leaders. But inwardly, I was competitive and sat among groups of ministers, judging their faults and weaknesses and wondering why I was not as favored as they appeared to be. So the law of sowing and reaping, giving and receiving continued in its effect—and you usually reap a lot more than you sow. Though I had a life of absolute integrity and moral propriety, my life and ministry came under judgment, and our reputation and finances suffered greatly. It all seemed very unjust to me and just fueled more accusatory thinking, but I kept my smile and polite tone with all those around me! I began receiving from others what I was giving to others in my thought life and conversations with my wife. The rigid scrutiny I gave others, others began to give me, and there were many faults they could focus upon, though I could see few within myself. There is nothing easier than self-deception.

> Pursue peace with all men, and the sanctification without which no one will see the Lord. See to it that no one comes short of the grace of God; that no root of bitterness springing up causes trouble, and by it many be defiled.
>
> —HEBREWS 12:14–15

Unknowingly, I was falling short of the grace of God, and it brought great trouble to my life, family and ministry when I defiled myself through my competitive and accusatory thinking. Even though in many ways the conclusions I had drawn were right, my attitude had unconsciously brought me into agreement with Satan, and he made sure that I received, good measure, pressed down, shaken together, running over—by my standard of measure it was measured back to me in return.

THE HEAVY PRICE FOR BEING RIGHT

Most people don't realize the consequences of judging others by a higher standard than they judge themselves. When you practice a lifestyle of the need to be right and the love of law, you begin walking down a path of self-defilement that will eventually lead to isolation and an inability to maintain healthy, intimate relationships. These steps may seem gradual, so it is important to be aware of them when you are beginning to stray from living by the law of love and grace. For preventive measure, allow me to share the pattern that I once followed.

1. Negative attitudes

The first thing that I did when I chose being right over having relationship was to foster a negative attitude toward those who did not think and act like me. I began to focus more on the faults of others than imparting to them God's grace and unconditional love. Without even becoming aware of it, I became self-righteous and hypocritical, using one standard to judge other people and a different one to judge myself. Eventually, my whole outlook on life and ministry became critical and cynical—I had taken the first step to defiling myself. Others didn't defile me. I chose that route myself with my accusatory thought life.

- What patterns do you notice in your own thought life? Are you constantly exasperated by the perceived shortcomings of other people? Do you notice yourself becoming more critical of your pastor, other ministers, your boss, coworkers, friends or family members in your thoughts? Do you consider yourself "better" than most people that you meet?

2. Impure motives

Once I spent a lot of time replaying in my thought life how others seemed more favored than I was, how others did not have the revelation that I had, how this person had done that to me and that person hadn't done this for me, it began to build an attitude (a habit structure of thinking) that unconsciously affected the motivations of my heart. My primary motive in ministry was no longer to help others and spread God's kingdom of love on the earth; I became motivated out of my own self-righteousness; the good works and hyperreligious activity helped me prove to myself that I had greater maturity and revelation than others. This all overflowed into my motives with family. I came home wanting everyone to meet my needs instead of living to make the Father's love known to them.

- What is behind the motivation for your service to others? Do you take an unhealthy pride in your accomplishments in the ministry or in charitable organizations? Do you look down at other people who do not perform as many good deeds as you do? Is your service leaving you with an angry edge at home?

3. Defilement of speech

The attitudes of my heart soon began to affect my conversations about others. "Out of the abundance of the heart the mouth speaks" (Matt. 12:34, NKJV). I knew better than to criticize or gossip about others outwardly, but beneath my words was often a devaluing undertone. I didn't defend people and point out their good when people were exposing others' weaknesses. Subtly demeaning or devaluing others was my way of proving my own self-righteousness and making me look good.

- Think about the words that you speak. What is it that you are communicating to other people? Do you find yourself demeaning other people when they happen to come up in a conversation? Are your words critical, or do you defend and help to point out the good in the person?

4. Divisive actions

Once I could no longer speak words of honor about a person, it was not long before my actions unknowingly began to follow the same destructive path. It became those who think like me against those who don't. I began drawing people to my side with subtle innuendoes that others were not as mature or had as much understanding as I did. I could not even see myself doing it. I was not aware that I was creating an environment of distrust, rivalry and strife among the people around me.

- When you encounter someone who does not live up to your expectations, how do you treat them? Do you intentionally avoid them or shun their company? Do you create an atmosphere of trust, or do conversations develop that help you convince others how much wiser you are than they are?

5. Damage to relationships

My focus on truth and being right rather than love and grace began to create a loss of intimacy at home. The negative attitudes I developed toward others were taken home in my relationships with my wife and children. I had to be right, and it left my wife and children with a tremendous fear of failure and rejection around me. Of course, this began overflowing into their other relationships. Though God has radically transformed my life and restored my family to me, they are still walking out the healing process for the strongholds of fear and insecurity that developed in them during those years.

- How are your relationships with your family members, friends and other people? Are you developing vibrant, caring relationships based on intimacy and trust, or are those closest to you obeying you out of fear? Do your children constantly strive to please you, but never receive your approval? Are you expressing your love to those around you in ways that they can understand?

6. Isolation

The final result of my lifestyle was perhaps the saddest of all. Many people just didn't enjoy being around me. I was too intense and driven to be right. I was not able to be home for my family even when I was home. It was difficult for some people to receive my ministry because it had such a hard edge to it. You had to pay a price of striving for perfection (no rest and security) to be around me. So only those very secure in God's love or those who could maintain such a rigid standard of excellence befriended me. I thank God for the few people who were secure enough to stand by me and who were willing to speak the truth in love to me, even though it took years for me to appreciate it.

- How many true friends do you really have? Do you feel that people are constantly rejecting you? When they do reject you, do you shrug it off, telling yourself that it doesn't matter because they weren't good enough for you anyway? Are your spouse and family members really present in their relationship with you, or is emotional distance beginning to take its toll?

The price for always having to be right is high, and the consequences can be tragic. Marriages fail, families are destroyed, and relationships are ruined, all because of the deceptive allure of self-justification, self-righteousness and the need for self-vindication. There is a higher place to which the Father wants His children to aspire, a higher place than being right. Placing the law above grace results in a vicious cycle that will only sabotage the very thing that all human beings are searching for: intimacy with God and with others.

THE GREATEST PRICE OF ALL

While one tragic consequence of always having to be right is isolation and loss of relationships with other people, there is an even costlier result of such a lifestyle: the loss of intimate relationship with the heavenly Father and entering into His rest. Dwelling in the Father's embrace requires an attitude of humility, of admitting our failings and shortcomings to God and others and asking for their forgiveness.

> Clothe yourselves with humility toward one another, for God is opposed to the proud, but gives grace to the humble. Humble yourselves, therefore, under the mighty hand of God, that He may exalt you at the proper time, casting all your anxiety upon Him, because He cares for you.
>
> —1 PETER 5:5–7

Experiencing the Father's embrace goes hand in hand with loving, not judging, our neighbors. We begin to enter into the realm of God's grace when we are willing to humble ourselves in His presence and with others, admit our sins and accept His free gift of unconditional love. Proverbs 29:23 tells us, "A man's pride will bring him low, but a humble spirit will obtain honor."

BEING FREE FROM THE LOVE OF LAW

Follow the four steps below to begin the process of being free from the love of law:

1. Choose to forgive each person who has hurt or disappointed you.

In a place of solitude, speak each individual name aloud and tell them that you choose to forgive them for the hurt brought to your life. Be specific. Personally, I have many times sought out people gifted in healing prayer to help me walk through the forgiveness process. You can go to our website and look up ministries equipped in healing prayer in your area (www.shilohplace.org).

2. Seek God's forgiveness for violating the law of judging.

Ask God to forgive you for each judgment you placed upon another person, each time you came in agreement with the enemy instead of with God's grace. Renounce every violation of the law of judgment that has been in your thought life. Yes, this may take some time. But it is worth it when you allow the blood of Jesus to cleanse you from all sin (1 John 1:9).

3. You may need to practice the principle of restitution.

If your judgment of others has brought harm to their life, often asking for forgiveness from God is not enough. For you to be healed, you may need to go to them and ask forgiveness from them. Do not mention their fault. Only take ownership of your own. Seek mature counsel on the best way to do this and on the choice of words that you use.

In 1997, as God was bringing me this revelation, I spent months going to each person, making phone calls and writing letters seeking for their forgiveness for my relating to them for so many years out of my own pain and immaturity. It transformed my life and resulted in a greater ability to make the Father's love known to my family and to the world.

4. Begin renewing your mind by casting down every thought and imagination that is contrary to God's grace (2 Cor. 10:4–5).

John Arnott's book *What Christians Should Know About the Importance of Forgiveness* helped me see the price I was paying for my choice to live by the law. I drew up the diagram on Law and Grace that is on pages 131–132 in this chapter, and I put it on my refrigerator, in my car and in the bathroom. I began making consciousness choices several times each day for my thought life to turn from law to dwelling in grace. When I first started this, 80 percent of the time my thought life was in law. Today, I believe that 80 percent or more of the time I dwell in grace. It has changed what I am reaping in my life, family and ministry.

You may want to begin a process of restoration right now by setting aside your pride and humbling yourself before the Father's unconditional love and grace. He is waiting with open arms, desiring for you to experience His affectionate embrace. If you need restoration and a fresh start with God, then I urge you to pray the following prayer aloud and accept His loving forgiveness and grace.

> *Heavenly Father,*
> *I come before You, so grateful for Your grace and unconditional love. Thank You for sending Your Son to pay the price for my sins. You love me the way I am, not the way others say I should be. I confess that I have not been walking in the lifestyle of Your grace, but I have been striving to attain righteousness on my own. My pride has stood in the way of my relationship with You and my relationships with other people. I have come into agreement with the enemy through my thoughts and attitudes. I have been*

critical and judgmental of others, and I now under-
stand the consequences of what I have done. I repent
of my sins and ask You to forgive me and cleanse me
of my unrighteous thoughts, attitudes and actions
that stand in the way of a vital and intimate rela-
tionship with You. I choose to forgive each person
who has hurt me. (List them by name and forgive
each offense.)

Father, please help me to have a right and correct
view of myself, to understand my own shortcom-
ings and failures, but also to view them through the
lens of Your love and grace. Help me to find my
sense of worth in You and Your love for me rather
than through my own accomplishments. I commit
myself to a lifestyle of love and grace rather than
requiring perfection of others. I choose to walk in
humility rather than pride; I choose to value my
relationship with You and with those whom I love
more than I value promoting myself and the need
to be right.

Thank You for Your patience with me. I am so
blessed to be called Your child. In Jesus' name,
amen.

QUESTIONS FOR DISCUSSION

1. Has there ever been a time when you held someone else to a higher standard of behavior than you required of yourself? How did that affect your relationship with that person?

2. Have you ever valued being right more than you valued fostering intimate relationships with others? What are some of the consequences that followed this choice in your life?

3. How can you learn to cultivate a greater spirit of humility in your heart?

Chapter Nine

Walking in the Light

Not too many years ago, I traveled to Slovakia to conduct a pastors' retreat for a friend of mine. While I was there, I had the opportunity to take a tour of a cavern formed deep inside of a mountain. My friend insisted that it was a sight I had to see. He neglected to tell me that it was a hike of 990 steps to the bottom depths of the river below! As we progressed deeper into the mountain, our tour guide turned on lights in each chamber we entered so that we would be able to find our way. The stalactites and stalagmites were awesome, but nothing that compared to the revelation that lay ahead.

Eventually we reached the particular cavern through which an underground river flowed. It was breathtakingly beautiful. Our tour guide told us that this river produced some of the healthiest water in the world. He said that people traveled from all over Europe just to come and drink the water that flowed from this mountain. The valley from which the river exited the mountain and flowed onto the land was one of the richest, most lush areas of Slovakia and produced the finest vegetables and fruits.

When questioned as to why this particular river was able to produce such life-giving qualities, the tour guide responded that it was because of the mineral content in the water that came from rich mineral deposits inside of the mountain. She then asked everyone to stand still, and she turned out the lights. For ten seconds, we stood in utter darkness. I could not see my hand in front of my face. When she finally turned the lights back on, she explained, "One reason this water is so pure is that nothing—no bacteria, no pollutants—live in the river as long as it flows in this utter darkness. It only produces life as it flows out of the mountain into the light!"

Revelation began breaking forth within me as I thought of how many Christians attend powerful conferences and experience deep encounters in the presence of God's love, only to return home and fall back into their habitual patterns of sin and shame. Others receive breakthroughs in counseling or prayer ministry, yet a short time later they can't seem to sustain an intimate and healthy relationship with God or their spouse and family. They end up just as harsh, unyielding and demanding with their family as they ever were, or they continue to perpetuate the same problematic struggles with intimacy and relationships as before.

When the tour guide said that the river only produces life when flowing in the light and not in the darkness, I realized that dwelling in a place where the Father's love is constantly renewing and restoring you to intimacy with others can only take place when we are willing to walk in the light of God's love. Fellowship with God is greatly hindered when we choose darkness over light.

> And this is the message we have heard from Him and announce to you, that God is light, and in Him there is no darkness at all. If we say that we have fellowship with Him and yet walk in the darkness, we lie and do not practice the truth; but if we walk in the light as He Himself is in the light, we have fellowship with one another, and the blood of Jesus His Son cleanses us from all sin.
>
> —1 JOHN 1:5–7

Not only is God's nature love, but He is also light; by His very nature God is against any darkness that lies within us. He is not against us. He created us for love; therefore, He is against any darkness that may hinder us from His love producing life and intimacy with Him and others. The very purpose of light is to set us free from anything that hinders deeper intimacy with Him.

LOVE, LIGHT AND DARKNESS

Unconditional love is never based on the performance or goodness of the person who is *receiving* the love. It is based on the nature of the one who is *giving* it. There is nothing you can ever do to receive any more love than you have already received from the Father; He has proven His absolute and unconditional love for you by the selfless act of His Son, Jesus Christ, dying at Calvary. God's love for you is not based on your performance; it is based on who you are in Christ, His beloved son or daughter whom He created for a lifetime of fellowship with Him. All you ever have to do is receive this love that the Father has for you.

Though unconditional love is free, it is a costly business. Accepting God's gracious gift and dwelling in intimacy will cost you everything, especially your pride. God's nature is one of love and light; He will love you unconditionally, but because He is light, it will be very difficult for you to choose to walk in darkness and maintain intimacy in relationships with God and others. I like the definition of *darkness* that Jack Winter taught me:

> Darkness is a moral state where you hide things, have secrets and give the enemy ground to traffic in your life.

Darkness is not just a place void of light. The fallen angels have been turned over to darkness. Darkness is also the dominion of Satan (Jude 6; Acts 26:18). Anywhere we allow darkness to remain can be an open door for the thief to come and steal, kill and destroy (John 10:10). The very thing the enemy wants to take from us is the very thing he lost—intimacy and fellowship with God. Darkness gives the enemy ground to traffic in your life and slowly to drain away a sense of intimacy, acceptance and love.

FOUR POTENTIAL AREAS OF DARKNESS

Many of the problems that I have had to deal with in my journey toward being comfortable with intimacy and love have been because for many years I was not that fond of the light. Let's be honest; I despised it because light is rooted in humility—a willingness to be known for who we really are. I wasn't too crazy about people knowing the real me. But darkness! Oh yes; how easy it was to hide and make believe and be unreal. That once was the real Captain Jack Frost, the one who loved the darkness that was rooted in pride, being more concerned with what man thought than with what God thought.

> And this is the judgment, that the light is come into the world, and men loved the darkness rather than the light; for their deeds were evil. For everyone who does evil hates the light, and does not come to the light, lest his deeds should be exposed. But he who practices the truth comes to the light, that his deeds may be manifested as having been wrought in God.
>
> —JOHN 3:19–21

Since 1980 I have had many experiences in God's power and presence. I became very familiar with handling the anointing and ministering in power to others. Yet I continued to struggle with bringing the presence of God home to my family and God's love restoring us to intimacy and love. Then in November 1995 I had my deepest encounter in God's presence. I spoke of this in chapter one. Before, when I had encounters like that, I would be humbled and would apologize to my family for being more committed to ministry than to them and for my inability to walk in tenderness and gentleness at home. But within two weeks, the sense of God's presence would drain away, and I would be right back to the place I started—struggling with intimacy and love. So once more I would end up seeking to find my identity in doing rather than being a gift of God's love to my family.

This time the conviction upon my heart and the brokenness and tenderness lasted about four weeks; then once more the hardness of heart and intensity slowly began to return. To have felt as if I had lived in a womb of liquid love for four weeks…to have seen my children risk opening their hearts to me…and then to feel it slipping away once more. Oh, the despair I felt as I saw the hopes and dreams of my children shattered once again as I slowly returned to life as the authoritarian father.

> For My people have committed two evils: They have for-saken Me, the fountain of living waters, to hew for them-selves cisterns, broken cisterns, that can hold no water.
> —JEREMIAH 2:13

I felt as if I had a broken cistern. I seemed powerless to live any other way but to be touched by God, my family have a faint hope that this time it would turn my heart toward home and then watch their hopes crushed as their hearts were broken once more as I returned to living by the love of law. For two weeks I pleaded with God for an answer as to how I could bear lasting fruit at home. Then on January 3, 1996, in the early hours of the morn-ing, God placed a key to intimacy in my hand, a key for which I had been searching for many years. It was a defining moment for my family when 1 John 1:5–9 exploded in my heart. I could finally see it. Lasting fellowship and intimacy are only possible when I am willing to bring all my sin into the light. I had been trying to cast out darkness through waiting for some great dramatic encounter when freedom begins with a simple willingness to walk in the light. That brings us to the first thing that darkness may be.

Hidden and unconfessed sin

Because I was so afraid of what others would think if they really knew me, I had kept unconfessed sin in my heart, areas of my thought life that I would not allow my wife or children to see. I'm not speaking of outward immoral sins, but the motives that drove me in ministry—the attitudes of pride, competition, jeal-ousy and envy; the aggressive striving to be somebody and to be seen and known. The thoughts and intentions of my heart that were all wrapped up in self-love. These were the hidden sins of pride and self-love that I struggled with most. I had a prayer partner I talked many things over with, but I was a closed book at home to my family. My darkness gave the enemy ground to traffic in every area that I chose darkness over light, and thus made it difficult for me to dwell in the Father's loving embrace.

> The night is almost gone, and the day is at hand. Let us therefore lay aside the deeds of darkness and put on the armor of light. Let us behave properly as in the day, not in carousing and drunkenness, not in sexual promiscuity and sensuality, not in strife and jealousy. But put on the Lord Jesus Christ, and make no provision for the flesh in regard to its lusts.
>
> —ROMANS 13:12–14

Light is an armor that protects you from temptation and burns away the flesh and its lusts. Only in darkness can pride defile us. So in that quiet early morning hour, I began writing down each of my sins against love, thinking that I would confess this to my prayer partner. But after completing several pages, I felt the Lord say to me, "After the children go to school this morning, I want you to sit down with Trisha and confess to her all that you have written down!"

"You have got to be kidding me! What would she think of me? She would lose all respect for me if she really knew what I was full of!" I reasoned.

God responded, "No, she already knows what you are full of. It is only in being honest with yourself and with others that this darkness that has troubled your family relationships will be displaced. Risk coming into the light, and then watch what My light will do!"

So that morning, after the children had left for school, for the first time in twenty years of marriage, I opened the deepest, darkest areas of my thoughts to my wife. She broke down crying and said, "How can the most holy man I know (did I have her fooled or what) be confessing his sins to me?" And she started opening up and confessing the darkness that was in her. Both of us began weeping uncontrollably, and God's love rolled in like a wave of warm oil pouring upon our hearts. For three hours we lay on the living room floor feeling like innocent little children in the arms of an affectionate father.

That night we repeated the process with our children, who were then seventeen, fourteen and nine years of age. I asked each one to forgive me for specific areas where my self-love and self-righteousness had misrepresented the Father's love to them. I could not stop crying for the next four months. I called it "oozing." I would just look at my children and begin weeping again; I would get on my knees before them seeking forgiveness for some act of harshness that I had committed years before. For four months I dwelt in a cocoon of humility and love, and God began restoring the heart of my children to me—a heart that had been closed for so many years.

The immediate result of choosing light over darkness was receiving the gift of humility and repentance (Rom. 2:4) that led me into a deeper experience in the Father's love and began restoring my heart to my family. Then right out of nowhere I ran full speed into the second thing that darkness might be.

Another's darkness invading our light

Darkness also can come as a result of wounding that we have received from others. It is not always a result of our own wrong moral choice; darkness can also be the result of our reactions to those who have disappointed or wounded us. Where unconditional love is, we often feel secure enough to walk in the light, but when we feel love becomes conditional, get ready to be blindsided. Unresolved conflict in relationships can be an open door to darkness. We are usually the ones who think we are right in the situation, so we think that our rightness justifies our negative attitude.

The one who says he is in the light and yet hates his brother is in the darkness until now. The one who loves his brother abides in the light and there is no cause for stumbling in him. But the one who hates his brother is in the darkness and walks in the darkness, and does not know where he is going because the darkness has blinded his eyes.

—1 JOHN 2:9–11

With the breaking forth of God's love in my family, a fresh anointing in ministry began to flow and increased invitations to speak began to come in. We had been a small, relatively unknown ministry, but now many lives are being impacted in the Father's love. Soon I was away ministering at three or four seminars or retreats a month; every time I did come home, I was totally exhausted. Trisha began to resent how once more the ministry had begun to take me away from her and the children, but she kept it all inside, thinking to herself, *How can I argue with how God is using Jack right now? But I do need him home more and more sensitive to my needs.*

I was neglecting my wife, but I couldn't see it. It was an area of darkness in my life that was affecting my spouse and family. My darkness invaded Trisha's light, and her darkness was about to invade me. Our darkness blinded us to the motives of our own heart, and we began to lose sensitivity to God's voice. Once that happened, we no longer saw clearly where we were going; we were being led by the voice of our own need. She needed more of my time, but I was feeding upon the thrill of being wanted and needed in ministry. Neither of us saw what was coming!

In May, I came home one Thursday from a ministry trip and was due to leave out Friday on another. Watch out, husbands, when your wife is quiet for a day around the house. Do not ask her this question an hour before you are to leave to go and minister at a retreat on the Father's love. "Trisha, is everything all right?"

The disappointments that had been building inside of her for months aggressively poured out as anger at feeling once more that I valued the ministry more than her. There was no way one hour was going to resolve this, and I left for the weekend with the conflict unresolved. I soon found out how quickly the sense of the Father's love can drain away. God's love never left me. It was my self-justification and need to be right that caused me to step out of the center of His love and into the backside of the desert. It is our sins that separate us from the sense of God's presence. He never leaves or forsakes us (Isa. 59:2; Heb. 13:5).

Have you ever noticed how often God uses your spouse to reveal the unyielded areas of your heart? Conflict reveals unresolved issues of pride, independence and self-love. This happens not only in family relationships; let unforgiveness and unresolved conflict remain in any of your relationships, and darkness slowly begins to creep back in, and you easily lose the sense of dwelling in the Father's embrace.

Trisha was right! No husband should be so busy with his job or ministry that he loses his sensitivity to the needs of his wife and children. I was right! No wife should try to get her needs met or her point across through anger or demeaning her husband. So for six weeks we hit the greatest stumbling block that we had ever had in over twenty years of marriage. Do you see how sly the enemy is as he tries to sneak darkness in on you? He wants to destroy intimacy, and he did a real good job of it at the point when my wife and I were experiencing the greatest breakthroughs in our life. For six weeks we went to bed each night with her lying as far as possible on one side about to fall off and me on the other side about to fall off. Don't laugh. You have been there many times before, too.

For over six weeks the desire to be right was much more important than the desire for relationship. Finally we could bear the pain of the darkness, anxiety and dryness no longer. What began the process of repentance was when we could see how much our darkness was hurting our children. Our nine-year-old son Joshua came to us and asked, "Are you and Daddy going to get a divorce?" Seeing the fear and insecurity on his face brought us to an awareness of our sin and back into the light pretty quickly. It took time, but both of us acknowledged our fault in the matter. We confessed our sin, and intimacy was restored.

When you allow unresolved conflict to remain in a relationship, it opens a door to darkness and emotional pain. You feel insecure with that person, and you start controlling your relationship with darkness. It can also open the door for the third thing darkness may be.

Our masks, cover-ups, walls and pretenses

> Light reveals; darkness hides. Whenever we do anything or say anything to hide what we are or what we have done, that is darkness.[1]

One of the greatest hindrances to intimacy is when we let darkness into our lives by being unwilling to allow ourselves to be known by God or by others. Light is silent, brings warmth and is a necessity for life. But darkness is cold and drives us to hide behind walls of self-protection, where we are unreal, or to pretend to be more spiritually mature than we really are. Our general proof of heartfelt sincerity before God and man is our openness and transparency.

Hiding the truth about ourselves from others, pretending to be better than we really are and wearing religious masks—these are the supreme sins that ultimately caused the Pharisees to crucify Jesus. The first sin disciplined in the Book of Acts was a sin of deception and cover-up. Ananias and Sapphira pretended before the brethren to be more spiritual, more sacrificial than they really were, and they died because of it.

Many people think they will be rejected if others knew the truth about them. There are those who will do that. But there are also many more who will value you because of your open heart. They will feel secure in your presence and know they can trust you because you are hiding nothing. Only in walking in the light do we experience the cleansing power of God's love that produces the lasting fruit of a transformed life. Bondages begin to be broken that may have hindered the flow of intimacy and love for a lifetime.

> For you were formerly darkness, but now you are light in the Lord; walk as children of light (for the fruit of the light consists in all goodness and righteousness and truth).
> —EPHESIANS 5:8–9

In a ministers' meeting where I taught on "Walking in the Light," a youth pastor received the revelation that he had been searching for as to why he had struggled for ten years in his marriage with a lack of intimacy and sexual issues. He knew he had to come into the light with his wife, so they went outside and sat in their car. He began to tell her of the lifelong struggle he had had with sexual issues and how it had affected his ability to walk in intimacy with her since they were married. Certainly it hurt her, and they sat for hours praying through the pain that surfaced.

Months later I received an e-mail from him telling me how that night transformed their marriage more than any other single event. He told how difficult it was for him to be honest with her and to no longer hide his guilt and shame, but the end result has produced a depth of intimacy that he never thought possible. She is now the one who is able to bring him the passion that he searched for all those years. He never thought he would be able to find such comfort and security in a marital relationship. It was the power of light that dispelled years of darkness and shame. That brings us to the fourth area that often opens a door to darkness.

The shame of past immoral sins

Once you step out of the light of God's love, whether through your own sin or from the mistreatment of someone else, you feel the need to bond to someone or something else because you were created for love and intimacy. Many times this involves immoral sexual activity. We must bond to something, but when inappropriate sexual behavior or impure lustful passions become the source of our search, we step out of the light into darkness. Sexual sin is a counterfeit affection that many of us have used as a substitute for the lack of intimacy with God and others, and it can leave us clothed with a garment of shame.

So many are seeking love in all the wrong places. Even if you fill a room with Spirit-filled believers, there will still be those silent cries being made all over the room: "Somebody love me." "Somebody give me the love I need." Somehow those people end up attracted to each other like magnets. Inside they are crying to be loved because the darkness in them stirs up the passions of the flesh. God wants us to flee from all sexual immorality, not because He is trying to deprive us of our fun, but because He knows the pain, despair and shame that can be the end result of such a lifestyle.

> Yet the body is not for immorality, but for the Lord; and the Lord is for the body...Flee immorality. Every other sin that a man commits is outside the body, but the immoral man sins against his own body. Or do you not know that your body is a temple of the Holy Spirit who is in you, whom you have from God, and that you are not your own? For you have been bought with a price: therefore glorify God in your body.
>
> —1 CORINTHIANS 6:13, 18–20

Sexual sin, more than any other type of sin, can wreak havoc in our lives because it is a sin against our very own bodies. The way we treat our bodies, our earthen vessels, will determine whether we will have a sense of value, honor and respect in our lives, or whether we will live lives with feelings of uncleanness and shame. When we feel unclean or dirty, it becomes difficult to love ourselves rightly. The darkness releases a sense of impurity and shame, and we end up rejecting God.

> For this is the will of God, your sanctification; that is, that you abstain from sexual immorality; that each of you know how to possess his own vessel in sanctification and honor, not in lustful passion…For God has not called us for the purpose of impurity, but in sanctification. Consequently, he who rejects this [purity] is not rejecting man but the God who gives His Holy Spirit to you.
>
> —1 Thessalonians 4:3–5, 7–8

When we have allowed darkness into our lives in any one of the first three areas—unconfessed sin, unresolved conflicts with other people or with our own masks and pretenses—we can then easily become cut off from our sense of intimacy with God. That lack of intimacy in our most important relationship often leads to problems in other relationships; we may become dissatisfied with our spouse and our minds start to wander, looking for love in all the wrong places. Men may become involved in pornography, struggle with the lust of the eyes or even fall into an affair. Women may begin to compare their husband to other husbands or even ministers that they know: "Oh, I wish my husband knew the things that Jack knows." "I wish my husband would minister to me the way that Jack ministers to his wife." If you do not think that your spouse is the greatest spouse on the face of the earth, then your marriage may be in trouble. Your spouse probably senses the dissatisfaction, and the lack of unconditional love can drive a wounded spouse even further away into deeper darkness.

Sexual sins can be devastating to your entire personhood, your spouse and your family! But even after you have asked for forgiveness and placed the sin under the blood of Jesus, there can still be a residual sense of shame. Every other sin takes place outside of the body, but because sexual sin is a sin against the body itself, the remnants of it can stick to you. You may feel the sense of shame, even in your physical body.

Sexual sin violates the first and greatest commandment: to love the Lord our God with all our heart, with all our soul and with all our mind. Pornography gives a false sense of intimacy; it is a seeking of comfort in the flesh because darkness has hindered you from walking in intimacy with your spouse and with God. These sexual bondages are often the most difficult to break because you feel too unclean to receive God's love. In an attempt to regain that lost sense of love, you may fall further into the sexual sin. When you repent of these sins, the Father will forgive you and wash you in the blood of Jesus, but the feelings of shame and uncleanness may remain if you are too ashamed for these sins to ever be known or brought into the light.

RESULTS OF WALKING IN DARKNESS

The blood does not cover what we leave hidden in darkness and refuse to uncover. "If we walk in the light...the blood of Jesus His Son cleanses us from all sin" (1 John 1:7). We can confess our sin to God, and He forgives us the first time we ask, but we can still carry the shame of our sin because of guilt and the fear of anyone ever finding out about it. This has the power to steal years of intimacy from our life and relationships.

My wife and I ministered to one woman who told us of how much pain and anger she and her husband walked in daily. For over fifteen years in their marriage she just could not fulfill his sexual needs because of the shame she carried. She told how they were both Christians and virgins before they were married; they were saving themselves for the wedding night. But one night she got mad at her dad and went to a bar, only to end up drunk for the first time. In a drunken stupor, she unwillingly ended up in a car in the parking lot having sex with a man. The next day she felt so ashamed. She asked God to forgive her, and He did the first time she asked. But she was too ashamed to tell anyone, especially her future husband. She ended up living in darkness. A few weeks later she learned that she was pregnant. The shame increased, and so did the darkness, even though she was already forgiven.

Forgiveness of sin and cleansing of sin are two different things.

Out of desperation she had an abortion. She asked God every hour of every day to forgive her, and He did. But because she chose to hide everything, the enemy had grounds to traffic in her life with accusation, self-condemnation and shame. The wedding day came. The husband who had chosen purity expected one of the best nights of his life, but her darkness invaded his light. The shame kept her from the wonderful joy that God had intended for that night. All through their marriage the sexual relationship suffered terribly and became a point of daily contention in the life of this sincere Christian couple. She was totally forgiven—but the power of darkness stole the intimacy and love for which God created them.

After fifteen years of pain, she heard me share on "Walking in the Light." For the first time she was willing to share her shame and pain with us. When our pain outweighs our shame, then we are ready for change. As she brought her sin into the light, the love of God wondrously washed over her, and she went home with the hope and faith to be open and honest with her husband. Late that night, she shared the experience with her husband. He broke down weeping, pleading for forgiveness for not understanding and for the pain he had put her through for many years. He took her into the bathtub and washed her from head to toe and anointed her with oil, praying that God would cleanse her from every sense of shame and uncleanness. Then they had one of the greatest nights of their life, just a few years late. The power of light dispelled the darkness and gave them a new marriage, and they began being used in ministry helping others who had been through the pain that they had overcome.

I believe that marriages must be built upon openness and transparency. But I also know that you cannot drive a 10,000-pound truck across a 5,000-pound bridge. Some bridges just cannot take a heavy load. Some marriages may have to start with professional counseling before you try to bring something to the light that is too heavy for the marriage to bear. It is wise to first seek counsel from spiritually mature individuals in the rebuilding of any fractured relationships.

CHOOSING LIGHT OVER DARKNESS

Unexposed areas of darkness can be one of the greatest hindrances to experiencing the Father's embrace. When we walk into a dark room, we do not cast out the dark, but we turn on the light. The light effortlessly dispels the darkness! For intimacy to flow freely in our relationships we must choose a life of openness and transparency. We need to be honest with our inward darkness before we are free to experience and maintain a life of true intimacy with God and with others. "Thou dost desire truth in the innermost being…" (Ps. 51:6).

> But if we walk in the light as He Himself is in the light, we have fellowship with one another, and the blood of Jesus His Son cleanses us from all sin…If we confess our sins, He is faithful and righteous to forgive us our sins and to cleanse us from all unrighteousness.
>
> —1 JOHN 1:7, 9

If there is an area of darkness in your life in which you may have received forgiveness but have not sensed the deep cleansing of the shame that you feel, you may want to find a trusted prayer partner to pray with you. "Confess your sins to one another, and pray for one another, so that you may be healed. The effective prayer of a righteous man can accomplish much" (James 5:16). If you know of no one, you may want to begin by praying this aloud yourself. Do not just pray it word for word, but be very detailed and specific about each area of concern. You can pray the following verses over each of those areas and proclaim forgiveness and healing.

> How much more will the blood of Christ, who through the eternal Spirit offered Himself without blemish to God, cleanse your conscience from dead works to serve the living God?…

Let us draw near with a sincere heart in full assurance of faith, having our hearts sprinkled clean from an evil conscience and our bodies washed with pure water.

—HEBREWS 9:14; 10:22

Heavenly Father, I come to You in Jesus' name. I thank You that the blood of Jesus forgives me and cleanses me from all sin and unrighteousness. I want to be free. I want every bondage broken in my life. I renounce the hidden works of darkness over my life and ask You to break any work of unrighteousness. I do not want to be bound any longer. (Pray as the Lord leads about the darkness you want to be free from.)

Father, You know how I have used my hands in unclean ways—wrong touching, the ways my hands have brought pain to others. I ask You to forgive me for sinning against my hands. Come and wash my hands clean in the name of Jesus.

Father, I give You my mouth and my tongue. You know how I have used my mouth in unclean ways— wrong touching, unclean speech, gossip, speaking evil of others. I ask You to forgive me for sinning against You, others and my own mouth. I renounce all uncleanness and darkness that came to me through my mouth. I refuse to allow it to speak or touch darkness again. Come and wash my mouth clean in the name of Jesus. (Be specific!)

Father, I give You my eyes. You know every way I have opened the door to darkness through the eye-gate—unclean things that I have looked upon, unclean pictures, pornography, lusts of the eyes, scenes of the past that have released darkness in me. I renounce those sins of darkness and ask You to for-give me for sinning against my eyes and against You, in Jesus' name. I refuse for my eye-gate to be bound by darkness any longer. I receive Your deliverance. May Your light cleanse out all darkness. (Pray over details!)

Father, I give You my ears. You know every unclean thing that I have listened to and that has defiled me through the ear-gate. Forgive me for listening to gossip and evil spoken of others. I renounce the darkness and ask You to cleanse the ear-gate through the blood of Jesus. (Be detailed!)

Father, You know how others have spoken words over me that caused me to feel shame, devalued, put down and rejected. I choose to forgive each person for the negative words. I renounce the power of those words and break their hold off of me. May Your love cleanse me from all defilement, in Jesus' name. (Be detailed about areas of concern.)

Father, I give You my mind, thoughts and imaginations. In Jesus' name, I ask You to cleanse me from all uncleanness and defilement that has entered in. I repent of opening my mind to ungodly beliefs, lusts, fantasies and ungodly imaginations. I ask You to forgive me and to cleanse my mind through the blood of Jesus. I renounce all open doors in my thought life that have led to darkness and oppression. I renounce the spirit of bondage and torment. I receive Your light flooding my mind and driving out all darkness. Cleanse my evil conscience through the power of Jesus' name. (Renounce the darkness in each area you are aware of.)

Father, I give You my body, that which is uniquely male or female. I ask You to cleanse my body with the washing of the water of the Word from all defilement and uncleanness that I have experienced from those who have used my body or touched me in unclean ways. I choose to forgive them and release them. I renounce any unclean spirit that others imparted to me. I renounce the power of darkness off of my body and receive Your cleansing, in Jesus' name.

Father, You know how I used my body to gratify my own desires in ways that made me feel unclean. I ask You to wash my body from all sense of shame. Wash my body from all unhealthy desires that influence me. In Jesus' name, I release all uncleanness and refuse to be bound any longer. Restore me to child-like innocence and a sense of purity.

Father, You know the love need that I have had. Forgive me for seeking love in all the wrong places. I do not want that pattern in my life anymore. I renounce it. I need a Father's love. I choose You to be my Father. I choose to be Your child. I need Your fatherly love and affection to come to me and penetrate my character and personality. I need You to take me into Your arms and pour Your love into me.

Father, I lift up my heart and hands to You as a little child would for his or her dad and ask You to come to me now. Here I am, Daddy! I need You! Take me in Your arms and give me the love my dad did not know how to give. Give me the love I have searched for all my life.

You can order through our ministry an audiotape series called "Healing Prayers for the Soul" that will help you to pray through many of the issues found throughout this book. See the back resource section for details.

QUESTIONS FOR DISCUSSION

1. Which, if any, of the following areas of darkness can you relate to and why?

   - Unconfessed sin
   - Unresolved conflicts
   - Masks and pretenses
   - Shame from past sexual sin

2. How have these areas of darkness hindered your level of intimacy with God or with others?

3. How can you bring these areas of your life into the light of God's love?

PROCESSING THE FATHER'S LOVE

Where then is a house you could build for Me? And where is a place that I may rest?...to this one I will look, to him who is humble and contrite of spirit, and who trembles at My word.

—ISAIAH 66:1–2

The abiding sense of the Father's love and the healing of our souls are not just experiences that come with dramatic encounters. We can easily put too much emphasis upon experience and then place too little importance upon our everyday choices and daily walk in the Father's love. Dwelling in the Father's embrace is often a process that is daily walked out through our interactions in everyday relationships. When Christ died on the cross and we accepted Him in our hearts, we received all the love of God that we will receive for all eternity in our spirit. Our spirits have been perfected in His love. This section will help you to learn how it is possible to abide daily in the Spirit through moment-by-moment acts of humility and love. This understanding is a must as we begin to pursue deeper depths in the Father's embrace!

Chapter Ten

Abiding in Love

I felt as if I had fallen off a boat hundreds of miles from shore and was left to swim home alone. I was in so deep that I knew I would surely drown. The daily anxiety and stress of a growing international ministry had finally built to the point of my breaking, and I could do no more. In my despair, I crawled up into my wife's arms and began to sob uncontrollably as words came out that I thought I would never hear me say: "I can't do it anymore! I can't be strong anymore! I can't be everything everyone wants me to be anymore!" What? Captain Jack Frost, the one who had many times overcome twenty- to thirty-foot seas in a forty-four-foot boat, is now acknowledging weakness? The one who, when others were lost at sea, somehow found a way to survive can't find his way now? The one who has always been strong and self-assured and could do anything he put his mind to can't take it anymore? He has finally come to the end of what he can do?

You see, since I cut myself off from my parents' love at about twelve years old, I have fought for everything I could get. I learned to isolate myself and be independent of needing anyone or anything. Just because I was saved and filled with the Spirit does not mean that the habit structure of thinking in my soul had changed. You can be quite a good Christian and even build a great ministry, and still not be able to trust fully in the loving Father to care for your needs; you end up taking all the responsibility and anxiety upon yourself. I had not felt like a son since I was a teenager, and even at forty-five years old, I still felt more like a servant than a son in God's eyes.

In the past when I reached the end of my rope, I would run off to a conference and get another shot of my Father's love. I found it so difficult to dwell in His abiding presence on a daily basis without regular dramatic experiences in the power of His Spirit. The demands upon me now were greater than ever before, and I needed a relationship with Him that was built upon more than just occasional crisis encounters with His power. I needed a loving Father's arms to crawl into daily so that I could cast all my cares upon Him. I needed to trust so much in His nature that I could daily believe that He was present to meet my need for comfort and nurture, even in the times I could not sense His fatherly embrace. This was a defining moment in my journey into dwelling daily in the Father's love. As the Father used my wife's comforting arms to impart His compassion and grace, I entered into the reality of the Father's words in Luke 15:31: "My child, you have always been with me, and all that is mine is yours."

Father longs for us as His children to enter into this kind of relationship with Him. He wants us to enter a place of faith in His goodness and love where we know deep in our heart that He is always with us seeking to meet our need as a caring Father, not just during times of dramatic encounters. It is in this place of abiding daily in His presence that His loving nature displaces our insecurities and fears and where we are being conformed into His image of love.

> If we love one another, God abides in us, and His love is per-fected in us. By this we know that we abide in Him and He in us, because He has given us of His Spirit…And we have come to know and have believed the love which God has for us. God is love, and the one who abides in love abides in God, and God abides in him…There is no fear in love; but perfect love cast out fear…We love, because He first loved us.
>
> —1 JOHN 4:12–13, 16, 18–19

We have all been created for love and intimacy. Yet many have been through so much pain that they have lost hope to ever be happy and to experience a healthy loving relationship.

You have longed for the instant dramatic encounter that you

have read about in previous chapters, and you may feel rejected because it has not happened to you. That is why making too much of the crisis experience can be one of the greatest hindrances to abiding daily in the Father's love. It then becomes very easy for us to wait on the dramatic experience for change to come and not focus on our daily choices to experience the Father's love and to give it away to the next person we meet.

I have found that people experiencing the Father's embrace can enter in two different ways. One is a way of great emotional release. The other is a way of humility and faith. Through experience, I have also learned that often those who never have an emotional encounter are those who, at times, are transformed the most by choosing to abide in the Father's love one moment at a time.

TWO PATHS INTO THE FATHER'S LOVE

My journey into the Father's love began as the "cliff diver." You've seen those guys on television diving off the cliffs in Acapulco or bungee-jumping off of bridges. Some of these guys are not playing with a full deck. Others have no fear. Some have a hidden death wish. I think I fit into the death wish category. I've experienced so much pain in my life that I became a specialist in giving that pain to others. I go for seasons living in "numb-numb-ville," blind to the pain my intensity causes in others. Then out of nowhere I get in touch with my hidden core pain, and all this emotional release occurs. My pain, which is plain to see by others, is all over me, and I have no choice but to jump. It's my death wish. Not physical, but a heartfelt grief over the fleshly things in my life that are bringing pain to others, and then a cry for the putting to death the self-love I struggle with. Then I get just crazy enough to jump off of anything into the arms of my loving Father.

Trisha, my wife, is a "wader." She is cautious and doesn't jump off of anything. She didn't go through the same kind of pain that I experienced in my youth. Her pain was more subtle and hidden.

She has to analyze and intellectualize everything first. Then she stands by the shore at the beach and waits for the tide to slowly rise. I'm out as far as I can go, crashing into the waves, while she watches and waits for the sea to wash around her feet. It is safer that way. She is not as likely to drown, while I come pretty close at times. Let me share with you an anonymous testimony of a "wader" and worship leader from Europe.

> Being a man of hard character, I did not know how to treat my soft little girl. I couldn't understand either why my personal example and perfect DNA did not bear fruit in her that would satisfy me. I could see God maturing and changing me in many areas, but it was very frustrating for me in my relationship with my daughter. She was the one I was always shouting at. There was not a single area of her life in which I felt she would act properly. Because of my disappointment and anger toward her, I could not see things reasonably.
>
> My pastor knew about this problem, and he took me with him to a conference on the Father's love by Jack Frost. I believe in miracles, but these American testimonies, so great and spectacular, full of dramatics or heroism—they are like super productions out of Hollywood. On my way back to the hotel after the first meeting, I had no doubts that what I had heard was profound and sincere, in spite of the dramatics and heroism. When I heard Jack's daughter's essay [found in chapter one], I asked God and myself, "What needs to happen in me so that I can experience something similar?"
>
> In the meetings that week I submitted to the "treatment" with humility. First, penetration of the childhood land, confessing my sins, forgiving the guilty ones, and finally the hugs. Yet I didn't experience anything special. Maybe it was because of my hard character or lack of faith. Months were passing by, and in all appearances nothing was happening to me. But one day I noticed that my daughter was pretty. Another time I was impressed by her sense of humor. So, after all something was changing. I cannot say what the

impact of the events at the Father's love conference was; God knows. But I mostly remember the essay—the most true and trustworthy testimony of changing Jack's heart into the Father's heart.

I'm aware of the fact that I'm at the beginning of my way. My daughter has been born again to me in my eyes. So we still have time for an essay. But apart from time there is also faith, hope and love. For my fortieth birthday I've just received a prophecy that God would put in me His Father's heart.

Too often we become addicted to the crisis experience and do not focus enough on our daily walk in the Father's love. You do not have to wait until the minister comes to town with the newest revelation and outpouring of the Spirit's power to abide daily in God's love. You don't have to sob and wail on the floor. Certainly those things can be of God. Expect a "cliff-diving" experience to come. Those times may come. But apart from this, daily you may seek and walk in faith, humility and love that begins to conform you into the image of your loving Father. You won't always feel God's presence. You won't always sense His favor. But as you daily submit your heart to His love, there is change taking place in your character, and you begin to abide in His love.

A little book called *Continuous Revival* by Norman Grubb has helped me understand how I can choose to dwell in His love on a daily basis and not just wait for a dramatic experience.[1] Abiding in the Father's love requires that we focus on three primary areas in our daily walk.

WALKING IN THE SPIRIT

Walking in the Spirit is a daily process that takes place moment by moment, step by step. It is determined by every decision that I make: whether I choose to focus on the things in the Father's heart and live in peace, or whether I choose to follow self-love and live in fear and insecurity.

He condemned sin in the flesh, in order that the require-
ment of the Law might be fulfilled in us, who do not walk
according to the flesh, but according to the Spirit. For those
who are according to the flesh set their minds on the things
of the flesh, but those who are according to the Spirit, the
things of the Spirit. For the mind set on the flesh is death,
but the mind set on the Spirit is life and peace.

—ROMANS 8:3–6

There are days when I choose to walk in the Spirit, and they are
so rich and full of a sense of peace and joy. These are the days
God's nature rubs off on me and I live to give His love away to
others. I love the expressions I see on the faces of my wife and
children when I walk in the Spirit of God's love. It is what makes
life worth living. By the end of the day, I am left with an overwhelming sense of the abiding presence of the Father's love, not
just flowing vertically from the Father to me, but also flowing
horizontally as I purpose in my heart to make His love known to
my family first, and then to others and the nations. What an
adventure! It is more fulfilling than in my younger days at sea
when I've caught groupers up to four hundred pounds or filled
my boat with nine thousand pounds of fish in one day on a hook
and line, making $4,000.

But, oh, the days that I am wrapped up in my own need and
self-love. Yes, I still have those days. And each one I have serves as
motivation to walk in the Spirit tomorrow, because the days of my
flesh are filled with aggressive striving, anxiety and hyperreligious
activity as I seek to find acceptance in the things I do. By the end
of the day I see my family's countenance fade to that of insecurity
and fear in my presence. I lie in bed at night seeking for the
Father's forgiveness and often rise the next morning asking others
to forgive me. This is what brings me back into a walk in the
Spirit—acknowledgment of each sin against love and choosing
not to live in guilt and shame, but to step back into the center of
the Father's love.

This is the key to abiding daily in the Father's love. It is not just in our past dramatic experiences. It cannot be a walk that is based on emotions, on running to a revival meeting seeking a new soul-stirring experience. Making too much of the dramatic experience can be one of the greatest hindrances to abiding daily in the Father's love. It is simply dealing with the issues in your life moment by moment, not waiting for a crisis to take place to seek God's face, but living with Him daily in all of the matters that come up, no matter how big or small. My definition of walking in the Spirit is moment by moment walking in humility and repentance and dealing with things as they are now, and not waiting for a dramatic experience.

> If you are living according to the flesh, you must die; but if by the Spirit you are putting to death the deeds of the body, you will live. For all who are being led by the Spirit of God, these are sons of God. For you have not received a spirit of slavery leading to fear again, but you have received a spirit of adoption as sons by which we cry out, "Abba! Father!" The Spirit Himself bears witness with our spirit that we are children of God, and if children, heirs also, heirs of God and fellow heirs with Christ, if indeed we suffer with Him in order that we may also be glorified with Him.
>
> —ROMANS 8:13–17

The enemy of our souls does not want us to abide in God's presence. It is in that place of humility and love that we do great damage to his domain. He has three basic tactics that he uses to prevent us from abiding in love: decoy, despoil and destroy. Satan seeks to *decoy* or distract us from focusing on our mission to make the Father's love known to others, he wants to *despoil* our inheritance that we receive in the Father's love, and he will try to *destroy* our sense of the abiding presence of the Father.

In my earlier years as a Christian, one of enemy's primary decoys that he used on me was the dramatic experience, one that either I had in the past or one that someone else had told me about. In those years I often hit rock bottom, and God had to take dramatic measures to rescue me and to save me from myself. Of course, I never forgot those feelings of overwhelming joy and peace that came when I experienced great breakthroughs. The problem was that I started spending much of my time trying to regain that feeling or waiting for the next breakthrough before I would walk in humility and love at home.

Then there were the times that I would see or hear of someone else's dramatic experience, and I would begin to think to myself, *What's the matter with me? Why doesn't God do that in my life? He must not love me as much as He does them!* Satan used the decoys of other people's experiences to deceive me into thinking that I was not favored by the Father. The truth of the matter, however, is that the most fortunate ones are those who do not have to go through dramatic experiences to walk in the Father's love. They enter in by faith, choose humility over pride, allow God's love to displace the fear and experience Him by faith every day—stress free! So what is the big deal about the dramatic experience? I've had many. I expect more. But meanwhile I choose to walk in the Spirit daily no matter what emotions I may or may not feel.

Satan's second tactic in my life was to despoil me of my inheritance. Even though I was a child of the Father of creation, the accuser of the brethren would constantly throw self-condemnation at me each time I misrepresented the Father's love to my family through being hard, accusatory or insensitive. I would get into shame, guilt and self-condemnation. Instead of acknowledging my sin against love and asking my family to forgive me, I thought I had to wait until I could receive ministry from someone else to be free.

The enemy's third tactic was to destroy my sense of the Father's abiding presence by trying to prevent me from keeping short accounts with God. When we fall into sin, we must immediately recognize it and confess it to the Father. Most of us prefer to walk with our sins rather than walk in the Spirit. But a daily walk with God requires us to guard our heart and thoughts and take care of any sins against love moment by moment as they arise, not waiting until the next church service to repent. If we have misrepresented the Father's love to another person during a time when we are walking in the flesh, a return to the Spirit is very simple. Go to the one you have hurt, acknowledge your sin, ask them to forgive you, and ask God to forgive you. You are then cleansed of your sin and restored into the Father's love. You simply enter in by humility and faith.

The blood of Jesus covers our sins, not our excuses. Do not excuse the present by looking back to the past or by waiting for future dramatic experiences. The true crisis experience is whether we will follow the way of pride and justification of our sin—trying to prove ourselves innocent by pointing out everyone else's faults—or will we choose the path of humility, confession and repentance. We cannot excuse our own sin against love by what others do. Do not justify your present walk by things that have happened in the past. Keep short accounts with God. Continually bathe in the cleansing blood of Christ through walking in the light and confessing each sin against love.

HUMILITY BEFORE GOD AND MAN

The second aspect of abiding daily in God's love is living a life of humility before man and God. Andrew Murray once said, "Humility before God is best measured by our humility before man."

The Christian walk is a walk of humility. It is the way to our salvation. It is our way to intimate relationships. Humility is the way to dwelling in the abiding presence of the Father's love. The number one hindrance to an intimate walk with God, one in which we truly know and are truly known by Him, is the absence of humility. When we are more concerned with what other people think than with what God thinks of us—that is the absence of humility. When we justify our behavior, shift blame, accuse, find fault, criticize or seek to vindicate ourselves—that is the absence of humility. When we had rather be right than have relationship—that is the absence of humility. When we do not confess our sins and our failures to others—that is the absence of humility. When we do not acknowledge our sins against love to the Father—that is the absence of humility. When we do not daily admit our desperate need for God to father us and help in our lives—that is the absence of humility. The absence of humility is the sin that caused Lucifer to lose the place of abiding in God's love, the Father's house.

> Clothe yourselves with humility toward one another, for God is opposed to the proud, but gives grace to the humble. Humble yourselves, therefore, under the mighty hand of God, that He may exalt you at the proper time, casting all your anxiety upon Him, because He cares for you.
>
> —1 PETER 5:5–7

Humility involves letting go of our pride and will and becoming like Jesus in the Garden of Gethsemane when He cried to the Father, "Take this cup away from Me; nevertheless not My will, but Yours, be done" (Luke 22:42, NKJV). God is opposed to anything within us that lacks humility, anything not humbled in our lives. Any area in which we lack humility will not have His life and grace flowing through it. A humble willingness to be known as we really are reveals a heart of sincere repentance and hunger for God. Anything other than that is usually rooted in the sin of pride, a sin against love.

Before I had a revelation of God's light and before I was living my life to receive His love and give it to the next person I meet, my excuses and self-justification for much of my "respectable Christian behavior" and negative attitudes went something like this:

"I've got to keep my walls up, or somebody will hurt me again." No, that's called the sin of independence.

"Well, if I am real, open or transparent, people will begin to reject me. They won't want to get to know the real me."

No, that's called the sin of pride.

"I'm just so tired. When I get home from work, I am worn out. I have just given too much of myself away to others; that's why I have been impatient and unloving."

No, anything unloving is a sin against love.

"You don't know what I've been going through at work. I am stressed out, and I just don't feel like talking after I get home."

No, that's the sin of separation.

For many years I had all of these little pet excuses for the barriers that I put up, for why I didn't walk in God's love, grace and goodness.

"I'm withdrawing from you because I don't feel safe in your presence." That was my sin of isolation and self-love.

Sometimes transparency and brokenness is hard. It usually requires self-sacrifice. Proverbs 18:1 says, "He who separates himself seeks his own desire."

"You made me act this way."

"The children got the best of me, and I had all I could take."

"I have to protect myself."

Sin! Sin! Sin! And each of my little excuses took me further away from humility, thus further away from dwelling in the Father's love. He never moved, but my excuses and pride separated me from the sense of His affectionate love (Isa. 59:2). This way of blame-shifting and justifying has been a habit structure of thinking in me since my youth as I tried to avoid admitting fault and feeling broken or rejected. Here are three little keys that helped me to break the power of these stronghold and ungodly beliefs.

1. *I had convenient names and excuses for my sins.* When I chose to begin calling sin for what it was, that was my first step toward true repentance. I chose to believe that anything that steals the peace of God from my heart or misrepresents the

Father's love to another living thing is sin. Then this excuse no longer worked for me: "I wasn't raised that way. I never received much affection as a child." These statements may be true, but if I am not walking in affectionate love now that I am the child of the Father of creation, and He created me for love, the root of such issues is a sin against love that I must address.

2. *I used to seek ways to cover up my sin deliberately.* I attempted to make myself look better than others by pointing out their faults, the speck in their eye, rather than dealing with the log in my own. Then I added hypocrisy to my list of offenses and hid behind a pretense of false righteousness. To be free, I began to recognize that anything I hide from others in order to make me look good is darkness, and I start drifting away from dwelling in the Father's love. I think I will start choosing the light!

3. *I deceived myself.* For someone with my history of pride and self-justification, I do not think there is anything much easier than self-deception. Once I reject the first two points above, I begin to deceive myself; eventually I am unable to recognize sin in my own life at all. First John 1:8 tells us that "if we say that we have no sin, we are deceiving ourselves." How often I have done just that. So to protect myself from me, I have given my family and several respected people in the Lord permission to speak the truth to me about what they see going on in me. I have asked them to ask me the hard questions: "How is your relationship with your wife? How are you relating to your children? Are you moving back into aggressive striving in ministry or intensity at home?"

> How often they are there to lovingly help bring
> me back to the center of the Father's love. I can't
> say I always appreciate it at first, but in the long
> run it saves me a lot of pain and shame.

This is a personal revelation of sin that the Holy Spirit brought to me. It is God's love for me that has helped me to see what I am full of. The accuser accuses me when I sin against love, but the Comforter comforts; it has become so easy to determine which voice is speaking to me. One produces shame; the other desires to restore me to intimacy and love. When I focus each day on walking in the Spirit, God's grace and mercy gently bring those things into focus that I need to confess and receive forgiveness and cleansing. And then the choice is up to me: I can choose either to live in pride or to walk in humility before God and man. My choice determines the kind of day my family and I will have. That brings us to the third area that helps me to live a life abiding daily in God's love.

TRANSPARENT WITNESSING

It is not enough to just get my sins right with God so that I can have intimacy with Him and at home. What God is doing in me belongs to my neighbors, the people with whom I work, the one I sit next to on the plane and the nations of the earth. My sins against love were not committed privately without affecting someone I know or love. I have chosen to live as if every conversation I have, as if everything I do either blesses or defiles someone else. Even if I do not speak to the person next to me on the plane, my posture, my countenance and my attitudes either testify of God's love or my self-love. Genuine repentance in my heart will be walked out in my daily life by my past defeats becoming God's victories in someone else's life. Abiding continually in the Father's love means that I am not only receiving the blessings and benefits of His household, but I am also ready at all times to witness of God's personal dealings with me and my struggles.

Three things happen when I am real, open and transparent about how God has dealt with me and the sin in my life. First, I become more sensitive to the shame that a particular sin brings. Confessing to others a past area of sin in my life becomes a catalyst to prevent me from ever committing that sin again. I used to struggle with the lust of the eyes, and I kept it to myself for many years. Finally, God began bringing a level of freedom to me, and as I began to share with other men how God had helped me overcome that particular sin, I realized that I never wanted to fall into that sin again. I came to a place of humility in that area and understood how great the grace of God was that covered my sin.

Second, transparent witnessing released a deeper cleansing and freedom from sins in my life. As long as I kept my sins hidden, only confessing them to God, I didn't become sensitive to them; they easily sneaked up on me before I knew it. But as I began sharing with others how God was delivering me from certain areas, I experienced a deeper cleansing process each time that I shared. Even while writing this book with transparent witnessing, at one moment I broke down weeping in my wife's arms at the very thought of how God's love has set me free. As my tears of heartfelt gratitude took me into deeper cleansing, I also moved into a deeper experience in God's love and in the love of my wife.

The third benefit that takes place as I share an area of past bondage or where I habitually sinned against love is that other people begin to recognize the sin in their own lives and come under deep personal conviction. As I have shared my journey in this book, how often have you been convicted of sins against love in your own life? Do you now see how it works? The honesty and openness of another believer who is admitting past sins and testifying of the Father's love delivering and restoring him will do more to bring someone into acknowledgment of their sin and into repentance than a hundred hellfire-and-brimstone sermons ever will. Transparent witnessing must be done with discretion, of course; you should only share those areas where you are an overcomer. An overcomer is one who overcomes more than he or she is overcome. That is, 51 percent or more of the time you have victory in that area. Be sensitive and led by the Holy Spirit for the proper time and place to share your heart.

TEN STEPS TO REVIVAL

True revival is not a series of meetings, but true revival takes place in the hearts of the people when they begin to receive a true conviction of their sin and cry out to God for His forgiveness, mercy and grace. This results in His children seeking His face, craving for intimacy to be restored with God and man and committing to a daily walk in the Spirit. The path to revival begins with just that: children of God learning to abide in the presence of the Father's love and then willing to give it away to the next person they meet. Revival usually follows this type of progression:

1. You begin to become more and more sensitive to the small, daily sins that gradually steal your ability to walk in love, joy, peace and the sense of God's presence.

2. You begin to recognize that every misrepresentation of God's love to another individual is an area of sin and darkness in your life.

3. You start confessing your sin as soon as you recognize it instead of hiding it, justifying it or attempting to cover it up.

4. You experience forgiveness and cleansing through the blood of Jesus Christ.

5. You feel clean and free, and gratitude fills your heart for what God has done for you.

6. You experience an overwhelming sense of God's abiding presence, and you begin walking daily in the Spirit. You don't have to chase after a dramatic

experience, for by faith, each day you have a sense
that you are drawing nearer to the Father.

7. You become so full of God's love and the joy of
   His presence that you can't wait to tell others. You
   become an honest, open, transparent witness for
   what God has done for you.

8. Through your transparent witnessing, others
   become convicted of their own sin and begin to
   desire an intimate relationship with God as well.

9. They confess their sins, repent and receive God's
   forgiveness and cleansing; they then become
   transparent witnesses themselves.

10. True revival is released within your family, the
    church, the city, the nation and the world.

If you need a renewed sense of the Father's presence in your
life and wish to recommit yourself to a daily walk with Him, then
pray this prayer:

> *Heavenly Father, I ask You to forgive me of my sins.
> I long to experience life with You on a daily basis,
> not just in times of crisis. I confess that at times I
> have placed more importance on the dramatic expe-
> riences than I have on daily abiding in Your love
> and giving it away to others. I desire instead to live
> as Your child in Your house, learning from You each
> day and allowing Your character to rub off on me. I
> choose to draw near to You, Father, and as You fill
> me with Your love and joy, I am willing to become a
> transparent witness to others of Your goodness, grace
> and love. In Jesus' name, amen.*

QUESTIONS FOR DISCUSSION

1. Are you walking in the Spirit every day, or do you seek the dramatic experience to maintain your walk with God? Are there areas in your life that are hindering the abiding presence of God's love? If so, what are they?

2. Have you ever had an electrifying "lightning-bolt" experience with God? If so, how did it change your life?

3. Have you been a transparent witness for the Father and a catalyst for healing and change to your peers? How can you become more of a transparent witness to those around you who need to know of God's life-changing power and love?

Chapter Eleven

Walking in the Spirit

I n 1988, Trisha and I participated in a mission trip on a medical boat that ventured up the Amazon River. We provided dental and medical services on the sixty-five-foot boat to the people of Brazil. People would row out in their canoes to meet us. But the Brazilians on the river are a generous people, and they wouldn't take anything for free. Every person who received our services left a gift: Some left fruit, others left vegetables, and one person left me these things that looked like coconut shells without the husks.

I had never seen anything like it, and so I asked the captain of our boat, "What in the world is this?"

He replied excitedly, "Wait till you see what's inside of it!"

He gave me a hatchet and told me to go up on the bow of the boat and hit it with the blade. It would split apart, and I would have whatever was inside.

I did as he said: I went to the bow of the boat, laid the strange fruit on top of the steelhead on the anchor chute, swung back with my hatchet and smashed down on it as hard as I could. Nothing! The hatchet just bounced right off.

I looked to see my friend laughing. "I was just kidding you!" he said when he could breathe again. "Here. Take the hammer. Try hitting it with a hammer."

So I tried opening it with the hammer, and again, nothing happened. As hard as I tried, I couldn't get inside to the fruit that lay within. I didn't even know what it was. My friend couldn't stop laughing, but I was getting a little annoyed. Finally, he took a razor-sharp machete and said he would show me how it was done.

He took the round shell, placed it on the side of the boat, got a firm grip and started shaving at it with the machete. Sliver by sliver, it started opening up, until there was a hole the size of a dime, and then the size of a quarter, and finally, the size of a half-dollar. My friend lifted up the thick shell and shook it; out of the hole came twenty Brazil nuts.

These huge shells grow in trees that reach mammoth proportions. The natives often build their villages underneath the trees because of the shade they provide. But the problem is that when the nuts ripen, they fall off the limbs of the trees from a hundred feet in the air without warning. The shells are so large that they cause all sorts of damage: Holes are punched in thatched roofs, children get concussions, and sometimes people are even killed by these shells that carry such rich fruit inside.

But when we began to eat those Brazil nuts out of the shell, it was like eating candy. They were so moist and sweet. I have never tasted nuts like these in my whole life.

Over the years, I've thought many times about how much I have been like the Brazil nut. In Christ I am a new creation whose spirit is made new in God's image (2 Cor. 5:17). At the core of my being (my spirit) I was created for people to taste of God's love flowing through me. But outside I was as hard as a Brazil nut. Those who dwelt under my roof without warning were in danger of being crushed by my intensity and harsh legalism. They would be left bruised and wounded by my hardened outer shell (my soul).

As a husband and father, my life is meant to provide a safe and comforting environment for my family. God has commissioned me with His love and filled me with His Spirit so I can love my wife as Christ loved the church and raise my children with nurture, affection and expressed love. For many years, they opened their hearts in hopes up getting inside of me to the tender place where they could feed off of my love. But too often, their tender hearts would just bounce off of the thick, rugged exterior, unable to get past my outward man. They would be left disappointed, receiving it as rejection; and I would be left feeling like a failure, justifying my actions, and unable to express the love that my family so desperately needed.

Because I carried so much hidden guilt and shame over this one reality, I believe it was difficult for me to receive a personal breaking forth of the Father's love in some of my deepest areas of need. For me to have the breakthroughs that I have written about, first, my heart had to be prepared through the revelation of walking in the Spirit that I received in the early 1990s from the ministry of Clark Taylor, a pastor from Australia, and Watchman Nee's book *The Release of the Spirit*. These sources helped me to discover who the real me was and to separate the outer man from the inner man.

BODY, SOUL OR SPIRIT: WHICH IS THE REAL YOU?

We were created in the image of God, who is Himself a trinity: Father, Son and Holy Spirit. Each of us is a triune being, made up of a body, a soul and a spirit. The body is our physical makeup, the temple of the Holy Spirit in which our spirit and soul dwell. Like the Brazil nut, each person is made up of an inner part and an outer shell. The hard, outer shell is the soul and is what can be wounded and can bruise or wound others. But the inner core is the spirit of a man, where God desires to dwell and cultivate the fruit of His Spirit. At the point of salvation, God fills a person with His love and takes up residence within that person's spirit. We become a new creation; the old things are passed away. Our spirits have become renewed in Christ, but outwardly our soul clothes the spirit and we must still address the pain and the wounds that remain in our outer shell—the mind, will, emotions and personality. Keep picturing the Brazil nut in your mind as we talk.

> Now may the God of peace Himself sanctify you entirely; and may your spirit and soul and body be preserved complete, without blame at the coming of our Lord Jesus Christ.
>
> —1 THESSALONIANS 5:23

Your inner spirit man is the part of you that was made in the image of God, and it is where God dwells after you have been born again. Your spirit was created for love; its most natural state is found in being loved and loving others. There is nothing more natural than for your spirit to receive and give love. However, your inner man is clothed with the outer realm of your soul—your thoughts, your emotions and your will—which rarely agrees with what your spirit tells you. It is this part of you that comprises your personality—how you feel, the manner in which you respond to people or situations around you. Think of the Brazil nut—moist and sweet fruit inside (your spirit) with a hardened and dangerous exterior (your soul). It is as if we have two voices speaking to us all the time: one gentle and loving and full of rest as it seeks to meet others' needs, and the other aggressive and driven to get its own needs met.

The outward man cannot accept anything that is spiritual in nature. The outward man cannot even discern spiritual things. To an unregenerate man, someone who has not received Jesus Christ as their Savior, spiritual things are complete foolishness. That is why atheists scoff at the gospel. It seems idiotic to them because they cannot grasp the things of God; they are operating out of their minds and not their spirits, and their outer man will lead them astray. Only the spirit of a person can understand spiritual things. When God created your spirit, He created you in His very own image.

> Then God said, "Let Us make man in Our image, according to Our likeness; and let them rule over the fish of the sea and over the birds of the sky and over the cattle and over all the earth, and over every creeping thing that creeps on the earth." And God created man in His own image, in the image of God He created him; male and female He created them.
>
> —GENESIS 1:26–27

> And we have come to know and have believed the love
> which God has for us. God is love, and the one who abides
> in love abides in God, and God abides in him.
>
> —1 JOHN 4:16

Because God is love, because my spirit was created in His image and because God's love dwells inside of me, there is nothing more natural on earth than for me to walk in expressed love, joy, peace, patience, kindness, goodness and gentleness (Gal. 5:22). For years I did not believe I had a very loving personality (neither did anyone else), but that was just my outer shell with all its walls of self-protection and not being comfortable with expressed love. On the inside, I loved my family and would give my life for any one of them. My struggle was getting the love I had on the inside to the outside and convincing my family that my love was real. My outer man would tell me that I am a real man; firm, tough, men don't feel; men don't cry; men don't allow themselves to get hurt; men do not show emotions or weakness. I seemed powerless to move past these ungodly beliefs in my soul and risk lowering the walls with certain people, especially my family. Any thoughts or feelings that are not at rest in love, affection and tenderness are not the real me. They are my unrestored soul. The real me is my inner man that is daily being renewed in God's love and empowering me to receive His love and give it away to the next person I meet today.

> Therefore we do not lose heart, but though our outer man
> is decaying, yet our inner man is being renewed day by day.
> For momentary, light affliction is producing for us an eter-
> nal weight of glory far beyond all comparison, while we look
> not at the things which are seen [outer man], but at the
> things which are not seen [inner man]; for the things which
> are seen are temporal, but the things which are not seen are
> eternal.
>
> —2 CORINTHIANS 4:16–18

One of the central keys for me to process daily the Father's love and then manifest that love to my family is in learning to recognize which voice I am listening to and choosing to follow today. Will I choose the gentle voice in my spirit (eternal) or the driven voice in my soul (temporal)? It involves making a choice to walk in what God has created me to be and to be renewed daily by His love, or to walk in the identity of my outer man, which is an accumulation of ungodly beliefs and habit structures of thinking that I have formed from all of my life's experiences, betrayals, disappointments, rejections and self-love. The problem I have often faced is that for too long my identity was in the latter and I really was convinced that that was the real me. The father of lies had very effectively deceived me into believing that I was the macho Captain Jack Frost with expressed love being unnatural to me, and that was more real than the truth that I am spirit and God has created me for warmth, intimacy and affectionate love.

WHO IS YOUR INNER MAN?

All of us were created to be a reflection of the Father's love, and God is at work transforming us into His image. His seed—His DNA, His genetic code—lies within us, and everything inside of us is being conformed to the image of love (1 John 3:9). When God took up residence in your heart when you were born again, He elevated your spirit to its rightful status. You were created to rule over all of God's handiwork; you have been crowned with His glory and majesty; your spirit was made to rule over all things—and that includes your own soulish realm.

> Yet Thou hast made him [man] a little lower than God,
> And dost crown him with glory and majesty!
> Thou dost make him to rule over the works of Thy hands;
> Thou hast put all things under his feet.
>
> —PSALM 8:5–6

When I came to truly believe that I was created in God's image—when I truly knew what His nature was like and that He was a loving Father and not an angry God—that is when I started becoming like Him. I began walking in a lifestyle of love, being renewed in His love a little more each day. Then my spirit slowly began to take prominence over my thoughts, emotions or desires that were not in agreement with God's unconditional love.

> There is neither Jew nor Greek, there is neither slave nor free man, there is neither male nor female; for you are all one in Christ Jesus.
>
> —Galatians 3:28

God created both males and females in His image of love. In the spirit realm there are no gender differences. I believe that tenderness, gentleness, affection and expressed love can be as natural to a man as it is to a woman. I can no longer justify being macho or unable to express healthy emotions and affection, because I know that I was created in God's image and there is nothing more natural for me than intimacy and love. The common belief that men shouldn't cry or show any emotions is a lie. I have the ability to be what God created me to be—a spirit being that can walk in the tender, feminine side of God's image, just as women can foster His masculine side. There are no male or female in the spiritual realm; I am created by the Father of creation in His image, created for God to flow through, created to do God things, created for love to flow freely through me. Every day I am being transformed a little more into a man who was created for the nations to experience God's love through me.

> Now the Lord is the Spirit; and where the Spirit of the Lord is, there is liberty. But we all, with unveiled face beholding as in a mirror the glory of the Lord, are being transformed into the same image from glory to glory, just as from the Lord, the Spirit.
>
> —2 Corinthians 3:17–18

When I first get up each morning, my first thoughts are usually all wrapped up in what others can do for me today or what others have not been doing for me (outer man thinking). If I stay in that mode of thinking, I will surely hurt someone that day. But after a few minutes of sitting in my study with a cup of hot coffee jolting me into reality and listening to some gentle music about the Father's love, I come back into reality. "This day is not about me, myself and I. That is my soul speaking. This is the day the Lord has made, and I am going rejoice that I can spend the day living out of my spirit and give the Father's love away to the next person I meet."

LIVING OUT OF YOUR SPIRIT

This is the revelation that changed my life: If I have accepted Christ and old things have passed away in my life and all things are made new in my spirit...if I am a spirit being...if I was created in God's image...if I was made for love...then how can I ever become any more spiritual than I am right now? In my spirit I have already received everything God has for me. I am never going to become more spiritually mature or perfect in Christ than I am right now in my spiritual man. My spirit is God's home. His unconditional love dwells in me. I have already received all of God's love that I am ever going to receive. God's grace and mercy live at home in me. The fruit of the Spirit is at home in me. The power of God that created the universe lives inside of me. His Spirit now lives in my spirit, and in Him there is no darkness at all. His love thinks no evil, and that love is resident in my spirit. Think about it; how can anything I do improve on that! There may be experiences I have when God's presence and love powerfully come upon me and break forth in my soul, but otherwise, it is more about His love breaking forth out through my soul to others than me trying to be good enough to earn more of it.

So why is it that for years I continued to struggle with sins against love, unforgiveness, shame, old wounds from the past, guilt and failure that hindered the release of God's intimacy and love? The problem did not lie in the area of my spirit (inner man). The problem was within my soul (outer man). I am given a choice each day: Nurture the pain, the past failures and the guilt, and I allow the temporal outer man to influence my daily life. Or I can release my spirit to take dominion over all those things and tell my soul that it has had its day, but now it is God's day. My outer man cannot mature into the love of God if left alone; it must be called into subjection to what God has created my spirit to be—a manifestation of His love to the world.

My outer man can never think a spiritual thought. There is nothing more natural for my soul to think about than going fishing or eating a piece of grilled salmon. But there is nothing more natural for my inner man to think than, *To whom can I demonstrate the love of the Father today? How can I lay down my pride and self-love and meet the deepest needs for acceptance and affection that my family might have?* There is nothing more natural for my renewed spirit than to flow in supernatural love. There is nothing more natural than for my soulish fears and insecurities to be displaced by the Father's love. There is nothing more natural than for the Spirit's power to be released through me to bring healing and deliverance to the oppressed. It is what I was created for! It is the most natural thing on earth! It is why God placed me here!

There are days that it seems completely natural for my outer man to sit back in my easy chair after a long day at work and say to myself, *I sure wish my wife would hurry up and get dinner ready. Why doesn't she come in here and wait on my every need?* That is natural for my outer man. But if I want to have a good week, I will listen to my inner man, and the most natural thing in the world would be for me to go into the kitchen, put my arms around my wife, tell her how much I love and appreciate her and ask her what I could do to help her and make her life easier. Then my life is much easier.

Ladies, it may seem natural to your outer man to think critical thoughts about your husband: *Why can't my husband have known what was in this book and written it himself? When is he going to wake up to the things of God?* But when you tap into your inner spirit, all you want to do is encourage your husband, look for ways to compliment him and to meet his needs and love him unconditionally the way he is.

I am never going to be more spiritual than I am right now. What enables me to dwell in love is to reach into my spirit and receive from the Spirit of God His love. The extent to which I am willing to humble myself and submit to what God has created me to be, my spirit created in His image, is the extent that His healing love can flow through me to others. As I sacrifice my self-love, my spirit will begin to burn away my flesh and God's love will break forth into other's lives through me.

WHEN MY WALK WITH GOD GETS HARD

When I first became a Christian, I experienced an outpouring of the love of the Father that touched my heart and changed me forever. But as I became involved in the church and began to learn the disciplines of the Christian faith, my soulish root system of performance made my Christianity one of the heaviest trips I had ever been on! I began to work at my salvation: praying, tithing, reading the Word, fasting, doing everything that I knew to be right. I exchanged the unconditional love of God for a lifestyle of my soul performing for love and acceptance. My outer man began to accumulate more and more guilt, self-righteousness, self-condemnation and self-judgment, because I could never do it good enough. My Christian walk got pretty exhausting! My outward man did its best to work at my spirituality. I was trying to make my outward man spiritual, and it became religion; the letter could not produce life.

Not that we are adequate in ourselves to consider anything

as coming from ourselves, but our adequacy is from God, who also made us adequate as servants of a new covenant, not of the letter, but of the Spirit; for the letter kills, but the Spirit gives life.

—2 Corinthians 3:5–6

Any time my walk with God gets hard, I know that I am no longer walking in the spirit but have begun living out of my soul. The inner man (spirit) naturally does spiritual things and thinks spiritual thoughts. The outer man (soul) naturally does natural things and thinks natural thoughts. As hard as I tried I just couldn't make my outer man more prayerful. My mind always wandered during prayer to thinking about playing golf or going fishing, and it left me feeling guilty. That is completely natural for the outer man. I couldn't make my outward man more spiritual. I ended up in bondage to the love of law and made my family miserable. During the fifteen years that I tried to force my outer man to be more spiritual, I ended up developing self-imposed laws and rules in order to feel that I was more spiritual so I could find acceptance in God. It resulted in the following pattern that brought great discomfort and pain to my life. Follow along this progression with me. Oh, you say that you have already lived there for a few years!

1. First, my childhood filter system of performance thought that through my rigid life of prayer, study and religious discipline and duty I was making myself more acceptable in God's eyes.

2. As soon as I left the way of grace I could not pray enough, study enough or do enough to ever feel accepted and loved by God, so I never attained the sense of closeness with God that I longed for.

3. So I worked harder at making my soul spiritual. I tried praying more, fasting more, doing more, being better.

4. After several years I got so weary and the Christian walk became so hard.

5. I began to feel guilty and ashamed for not being good enough and for so many fleshly thoughts.

6. I felt unworthy to be loved by God and that He had His personal favorites—and I was not one.

7. So I started making personal promises and vows to get closer to God and work harder at being a good Christian and fulfill all the religious duties that I felt were required of me.

8. I seemed helpless to fulfill all the personal promises that I made to myself to be more disciplined, so my level of guilt, frustration and anxiety kept increasing.

9. I lost a sense of value and self-worth in God's eyes apart from my performance.

10. I started treating my family and others the way I felt about myself.

11. My love became conditional. The disciplines and duties that I had to fulfill to feel loved and accepted by God is what I required from others for them to feel loved and accepted by me.

12. I ended up with most of my relationships unhealthy as I sought to control them in order to get my own needs met. There is no love in law!

13. I ended up in spiritual burnout!

How many laws have you made for yourself and failed to keep? When you fail to keep your self-imposed laws, you feel guilty and no longer feel close to God. When you do not feel close to God, you begin living out of the outer man, and walking in love is very difficult. Being a Christian can be a heavy burden or a joyful, peaceful walk. The secret of abiding in love rests on Christ, not on me. In Christ and in my spirit there is no striving, no drivenness, no anxiety and no guilt. When I have no guilt I draw closer to God because He is already dwelling within me.

> For by grace you have been saved through faith; and that not of yourselves, it is the gift of God; not as a result of works, that no one should boast.
>
> —EPHESIANS 2:8–9

MAKING YOUR JOURNEY EASY AND YOUR BURDEN LIGHT

> Come to Me, all who are weary and heavy-laden, and I will give you rest. Take My yoke upon you, and learn from Me, for I am gentle and humble in heart; and you shall find rest for your souls. For My yoke is easy, and My load is light.
>
> —MATTHEW 11:28–30

How can you position yourself to enter into God's rest and your spiritual man to rise above the outward man?

First of all, *agree with what the Word of God says about you.* You are created in God's image, and God is love. Every fiber of your being has been created for intimacy with God. We have learned throughout this book that God's unconditional love for you is never based upon your behavior but upon His character of perfect love and grace. Outer man should never be judge of whether you feel close to God or not. God's truth, love and grace are the only factors of proof of whether God is with you. You were born of the Spirit to be filled with the Spirit, to walk in the Spirit, to talk in the Spirit, to commune with the Spirit, to live as a spirit being and for your spirit to rule over strongholds. That is a greater reality than your outer man that is temporal and fading away.

Second, often *you will have to tell your outer man to be quiet!* Seek for peace in the inner man, not in the head. Your mind is to serve your spirit. The emotions are to be subordinate to your spirit. As soon as you don't "feel" close to God, tell your emotions to line up with God's Word. Tell your outer man to line up with your spirit man; allow truth to be your only reality. Do not go by feelings or emotions. Do not look to feelings of blessing to determine whether you are close to God. Anytime your emotions say, "God is not close to me. God couldn't love me. God can't use me," then your outer man is agreeing with the father of lies. The Father of creation has told you, "My child, you have always been with me, and all that is mine is yours…I will never desert you, nor will I ever forsake you" (Luke 15:31; Heb. 13:5).

There is rarely a time when I step into the pulpit to minister that I have not felt feelings of insecurity or unworthiness just before I walk to the platform. My outer man tells me, "Who do you think you are speaking to all of these people about the Father's love? Look at all the times you have fallen short of God's love with your family." I have to speak to those thoughts, "Soul, be quiet! I am spirit, and God dwells in me; by His grace He will minister through me." And when I step to the podium there is no fear or insecurity because I moved out of the soul and retreated into the spirit.

Finally, *choose to dwell daily in the Father's embrace.* The outward man seeks for the power of God to deliver him from his circumstances. The spiritual man seeks for the presence of God to fellowship with him and be with him through his circumstances. When I am overwhelmed in my mind or emotions and cannot seem to get in touch with my spirit, that is when I stop everything, go into my study and put on some quiet, soothing music about the Father's love. (Call Shiloh Place Ministries for CDs.) Then I lie on the floor before the Father and say to Him, "Dad, I am over here in my soul and can't seem to find You. Please help me." I don't pray a deep, heavy prayer, but just admit to Him that I need His help and then surrender to His love: "Father, draw me back into my spirit. Draw me back to You. I have moved over into my own thoughts, emotions, insecurities and fears, and I feel alone and discouraged. I need Your fathering arms to embrace me. Run to me to give me the love and comfort that I need."

Soon, the Father's love and peace come over me, and my focus shifts. I separate the outward man from the spiritual, and I step right back into the things of the spirit. Everything changes; my attitudes, my desires and my motivations all begin to realign with the Father's heart, and I am free once more to minister His love to my family and others.

Receiving the revelation of walking in the spirit is so important to the daily process of dwelling in the Father's love. Do you need to make a fresh commitment to walk in the spirit, to cultivate your inner man as you seek for the Father's love to quiet your outer man? Pray this prayer aloud:

Dear heavenly Father, I long to be a true worshiper of You, to worship You in spirit and in truth, to lay down all of my pretenses and commune with You, spirit to Spirit. Too many times, I have relied on my own thoughts or emotions in order to relate to You. Help me to step out of the soul, out of the outward man, and into my spirit. Release Your love through me. Help me to live, not under the burden of the law, but in the freedom of Your grace, under the shadow of the cross.

I commit to crucify my flesh, to cast down every thought and emotion that is not of You. I choose to quiet these thoughts and feelings. I choose to walk in the reality of Your Word and what You have created me to be. I thank You for who I am in Christ, Your beloved child, a gift of love to the nations. I draw near to You; draw me back to Your Spirit to that place of joy, peace and righteousness where I can receive Your love and grace.

Thank You for Your love and healing touch in every area of my life—spirit, soul and body. In Jesus' name, amen.

QUESTIONS FOR DISCUSSION

1. Describe a way in which your soul—your mind, your will or your emotions—has hindered your relationship with God. Do you have that area resolved?

2. Describe a time when you have related to someone—your spouse, a friend or a family member—through the outward man and it resulted in conflict. How would the situation have been different if you had related to them through your spirit?

3. What steps do you plan on taking in the next month to cultivate a greater walk in the Spirit in your life?

Chapter Twelve

Restoring the Heart of the Family

Experiencing the Father's unconditional love is all about choosing to accept our mission in life, what God has created us for. He has created us to experience His love and to make it known to our families and the nations. He has chosen this season in church history to reveal His affectionate Father's heart, because before every major revival there has been social crisis in the land. Then God brings a fresh outpouring of His grace and begins to meet the need of the social crisis. Revival results. Today, the social crisis of our nation and the world is fatherlessness. God is revealing His Father's heart to His children because it is difficult being tender, loving parents until we have experienced the affectionate love of a father's and mother's heart. As the Father's love meets our need, His love flowing through us can begin to meet the need of the crisis in the nations.

The American family is in trouble. Almost half of the marriages in America are headed for divorce.[1] The statistics of divorce are no different among Christian families.[2] Sadly, the church, as we have known it, has had very little impact to restore the American family to wholeness. Our children are suffering the consequences of fear, insecurity and low self-esteem, and they are crying out for their father's and mother's embrace. It is no surprise that rebellious attitudes, drug abuse, immoral sexual activity, out-of-wedlock pregnancy, gang activity and crime rates among teenagers have risen steadily as the deterioration of the American family continues.

What we need is a reformation—a radical change within the church and our families that will sweep across America and restore the hearts of husbands and wives to each other and the hearts of parents to their children.

My own family has experienced many battles and is still in the process of restoration and healing. We have known great pain and have struggled through difficult times just like many other families. We have battled against destructive habit patterns that seem to have been passed down from both sides of the family from generation to generation. In spite of my own pain and weaknesses, I am willing to pay a price to see that many of these unhealthy family traits end with me and are not passed on to my children and grandchildren.

Like many other households today, we were desperately in need of an outpouring of the Father's love. Fortunately, God is in the business of rescuing us from ourselves and the pain we often inflict on others. His plan in the last days is for the restoration of the family—for the hearts of fathers and mothers to turn back to their children, for love and intimacy to flourish between husbands and wives.

GOD'S PROMISE OF RESTORATION

The earth belongs to the Lord; God created the world and gave man dominion over it, but since the Fall, Satan has had far too much influence in the life of the family. He has done everything he can to destroy the Christian family and disintegrate the fabric of our society. But God promises restoration of everything that has been lost, and that includes the restoration of your family.

> All the ends of the earth will remember and turn to the LORD, and all the families of the nations will worship before Thee.
>
> —PSALM 22:27

In the End Times, there will be a great revival in which families from all nations will return to the Lord and receive healing and renewal. God promises that the hearts of the fathers will turn back toward the children, and the hearts of the children will return to their fathers. The Old Testament closes with the following passage that indicates how important the family is to the Father. He will release a supernatural move of the Spirit to convict the hearts of fathers to no longer seek for their identity in the things they do, but return to finding their identities in what God has created them to do—to manifest the love of God to their families. This manifested love will then overflow to the nations of the earth—thus the curse of fatherlessness will be broken off of the land.

> Behold, I am going to send you Elijah the prophet before the coming of the great and terrible day of the Lord. And he will restore the hearts of the fathers to their children, and the hearts of the children to their fathers, lest I come and smite the land with a curse.
>
> —MALACHI 4:5–6

Wherever a father's heart is turned toward anything other than his children, a curse can be released upon the family. Even Christian households can fall under deception when the priorities of the parents are not in line with God's priorities. In my own household, my heart was more inclined toward deep-sea fishing in the early years, and then later to ministry. I was blinded to the needs of my family, thus we lived under a curse, and the results were obvious: My wife spiraled into a deep depression, and my children were acting out their frustration in unhealthy and angry ways. I was oblivious to it all, because my focus was not on what took place at home; my focus was on building a reputation and a ministry so I could change the world. It didn't matter that I had a ministry that was touching the lives of thousands of people; I was not making ministry to my own family first priority, and my wife's and children's lives began to fall apart. We needed a restoration, a reversal of the curse that had been allowed to enter and wreak havoc in our home.

In the Hebrew language, the word *restore* means "to bring back to the point of departure, to turn from its evil way, to turn around, to return, to come back." When God begins to restore our families, He is bringing them back to the place they were before sin entered the world. He is returning our families to that point of departure. God wants to "restore" our relationships to the depth of love and freedom from fear and shame that Adam and Eve first shared before their sin and cover-ups brought blame shifting, separation and a loss of intimacy to the family. I want to reveal to you how deception works its way into a marriage and begins the disintegration of the family.

THE MOST COMMON MISTAKES IN MARRIAGE

When Trisha and I decided to settle down, get married and have a family, we had no idea what we were really getting into! It did not take long for reality to begin to sink in, and we began to realize that our marriage was not at all what we thought it would be. It seems we both got married for two different reasons. I got married for her to meet all of my physical, household and social needs. She got married for me to meet all of her needs for love, affection and intimacy.

Before marriage, Trisha's thinking went something like this: *I am finally going to marry my Prince Charming! Jack is so wonderful and sensitive* (certainly I was when I was trying to manipulate her to get my needs met)—*I can't wait to marry him. He loves me unconditionally, and our lives together are just going to be perfect. Well, maybe he isn't perfect right now. But after we get married, I'll see that Jack makes all the necessary changes that will meet my needs.*

Before marriage, my thinking went something like this: *I am so tired of the singles game. Trisha is such a wonderful girl. She does everything she can to meet my needs. She cooks for me, does my laundry, cleans my house; all my friends think that she is so much fun, and she is so affectionate and passionate. I think that I had better*

*marry this girl because there are not many girls out there that will
meet my needs like her.*

I wonder how many of you entered into your marriage or are
planning to marry with similar motives, thinking that marriage is
all about finding the ideal mate for you and getting all of your
needs met through your spouse? I have identified a progression
of sixteen major mistakes that Trisha and I made that resulted in
great disenchantment, disappointment, discouragement, depression and almost disaster. Many of these mistakes center around
basic myths about marriage that naive husbands and wives cling
to despite the fact that they are not grounded in reality. Part of
processing the Father's love in your family will be to identify
these ungodly beliefs, call them daily to the cross, submit to
God's love and allow Him to use you to begin the process of
renewal and restoration in your family. Ken Nair's book
Discovering the Mind of a Woman helped me see these mistakes in
my own marriage and the five-part scenario that follows. I highly
recommend it for any husband.[3]

Mistake #1: Believing that you will always be happy

Because Trisha and I felt that we were in love and because most
of the time we felt warm and attracted to each other, we thought
that we would be happier in marriage than remaining single. Of
course, that is the way it should be; no one should get married to
someone who makes them miserable. But we made some wrong
assumptions. It only took a couple of months for major problems
and disappointments to arise.

Mistake #2: Not understanding that your spouse has expecta-
tions of you

The first week that we were married, Trisha expected me to
come home as soon as I got off of the fishing boat so I could meet
her needs. But I was used to hanging out with the guys after work,
so instead of going straight home to my sweet little wife who was
going to be there waiting for me so she could meet my need, I

went off with my buddies to drink a few beers and to shoot some pool as I always did. How long do you think that Trisha went for that scenario? During two years of dating, life was pretty good, but after a few months of marriage we had serious trouble. We had no concept of each other's expectations in the marriage, and unmet expectations produce major frustrations.

Mistake #3: Not realizing that men and women have different needs

Trisha and I did not understand that as a man and woman, we had different needs, and we each expected the other to lay down their own needs to meet the other's. My needs at that time were all wrapped up in counterfeit affections and finding my identity in being "top hook" and Captain Jack Frost. I spent far too many hours on my boat preparing for the next trip to sea and then too many days at sea sacrificing my wife's needs so I could be "top hook." When I came to know the Lord and entered the ministry, I exchanged the sea for finding my identity in ministry. Because Trisha's needs were for quality time with me, affirmation and affection, she took my lack of attentiveness as rejection of her, so she became more disgruntled and hurt as she expected me to meet most of her needs.

Mistake #4: Keeping your grievances to yourself, hoping they will go away

In the early years, instead of airing her grievances and allowing us to find a compromise, often Trisha would just keep quiet, hoping that the problem (me) would somehow fix itself. Women who are raised in religious homes will often practice this behavior— they learned that it is better to avoid an argument and be a peacemaker than to let their feelings be known. But unfortunately, their feelings do not go away; they fester beneath the surface, and the problem grows rather than shrinks.

Mistake #5: Putting all your energy into hobbies and activities outside of the home rather than into the marriage

When my wife quietly began to distance herself, I followed the path that many men take when they feel they are not very good at intimacy and marriage: I gave myself to finding something I thought I could do well. I went fishing. It was very easy for me to become obsessed with that. When I went to Bible school, it was tennis. Then when I entered the ministry, it was that or even golf. Then I discovered the "warm fuzzies" that I could receive from people liking me in ministry, so I became more committed to ministry than to love. Rather than focusing my energy on where the problem was, I focused on something I thought I could do well, something that made me feel good about myself. Trisha found her identity in our children.

Mistake #6: Putting your own needs and desires ahead of those of your spouse

After a few years in marriage, all I focused on was my work. Most days, I was so exhausted when I came home that I had no energy left for my wife and children. I was so focused on my own situation that I began to see Trisha only as someone who was there to meet my needs and improve my own life. I became less concerned about her needs and more self-absorbed in my own.

Mistake #7: Not accepting admonition from your spouse, even if given in a loving manner

At first, Trisha tried gently to help me see that we had some problems, but I was not open to discussion or to receiving help. I received it as criticism. It is at this point that many women start to nag. Men, if you think your wife is nagging you, that is usually an indication that there is something missing in her life and you are not concerned enough with her needs. One of the greatest needs that a woman has is to feel a sense of value and acceptance from her husband, but most women don't share that need with their spouses because they can't take the risk of being rejected in such a sensitive area. Instead, they nag—it's not about the dirty under-wear left on the floor; the anger they are expressing is the resent-ment they feel at not having their needs met.

Mistake #8: Not sharing intimate details of your lives with one another

When gentle encouragement didn't work, Trisha tried asking me questions in order to reconnect with me and rekindle inti-macy in our marriage: "How was your day, honey?" she asked. Or, "What did you do all day?" I didn't like personal questions; most men don't. So why do women ask them so much? Life shouldn't be an interrogation every time we come home. Could it be that our wives just want to feel a part of our lives? By not sharing details of our lives with our wives, we shut them out, and they begin to feel excluded and unloved.

Mistake #9: Allowing hurt, anger and grief to pile up

Eventually, Trisha gave up trying to reach me, and she started taking everything I said or did as a personal rejection. Everything became an "event," right down to the way that I looked at her or something I said that she completely misunderstood or took out of context. Her pain had piled up inside of her to the extent that it began to spill over into much of our conversations. My response to the pain was "numb-numb-ville." Don't talk, don't trust, don't feel, and you won't get yourself hurt or in any trouble.

Mistake #10: Focusing only on the sexual aspect of marriage for intimacy

Because I was not communicating with Trisha and we had very little recreation time together or experienced any depth of emo-tional intimacy, I found, just as many men do, that the most important part of my marriage was in the bedroom. I thought that if that aspect of marriage was OK, then I could handle any-thing else at home. Lacking any other connection with Trisha, I began to want sex more and more often. With no intimacy, it was my only source of comfort and nurture, so you can imagine how she felt about that! She started to see me as "one of those men" who only want "one thing." She began to feel used and taken advantage of in what should have been the safest place for her: her own bedroom. Because of this disconnected relationship in marriage, many men turn to pornography to find the comfort and nurture they feel is missing at home.

Mistake #11: Placing a guilt trip on your spouse

As a good Christian with no moral failure, I came home every night and always said the words, "I love you." So I could not imagine what I was doing wrong. I concluded that somehow it must be Trisha's fault, and she concluded that it was mine. So we started laying subtle guilt trips on one another. I was living in "numb-numb-ville." I was good at closing my heart and not receiving love. But Trisha could not operate that way. Everything went straight to her heart and only made her resentment and bitterness toward me grow.

Mistake #12: Compacting your emotions until they explode in other areas

If you have a garbage compactor in your house and don't clean it out for a year, imagine how your house will begin to smell. Life can get pretty unpleasant when you stop taking out the trash. The same is true with negative emotions. If you consistently find your wife locking herself in the bathroom and sobbing, or if she criticizes you or the children for simply squeezing the wrong end of the toothpaste tube, there might be some compacting going on. Eventually Trisha could not share any of her feelings with me because I wouldn't listen or change anyway. But things just do not go away; they begin to come out in other ways.

Mistake #13: Turning your anger inward until it becomes depression

Compacting emotions too long can affect a person's emotional stability. I was not a safe place for Trisha to express her feelings and emotions, so she turned her anger inward. She went into a deep depression for a year. Part of it was postnatal depression. But it was also fueled by the emotions she had pushed down for seven years in marriage. For the ten years that followed, she had to fight to keep depression off of her door.

Mistake #14: Not acknowledging there is a problem

In the 1980s Trisha began to seek help from everyone she could find: pastors, counselors, even psychiatrists. But in my world, everything was fine. I was reasonably happy in marriage. I would go out and find my identity in the sea, and later in ministry, and come home every now and then for my wife to meet all my sexual needs. What do I have to complain about? I thought that any disagreements we had were my wife's problems. I often say now that I have been happily married twenty-seven years, and my wife has been happily married for seven years. It took a revelation of the Father's love for me to see how far I was from intimacy and how much pain I had caused my wife because I was uncomfortable with love and intimacy.

Mistake #15: Believing that everything is OK

I believed that I was more emotionally stable than Trisha, although in reality, she was in better emotional health than I was because she was in touch with her pain and emotions. I was in complete denial because I felt that I was so disciplined and did so many good Christian things. Someone once said, "There are two types of people on the earth: those with problems, and those in denial. And 'de-Nile' is a river in Egypt where people are held in bondage!"

Mistake #16: Refusing to take responsibility for any of the problems

As the husband, I now see that I should have taken responsibility for my wife's emotional health. Trisha was a wounded, depressed pastor's wife whose life was falling apart. When she tried to talk to me, I refused to see that I had anything to do with the problem, and instead of helping, I made the situation worse. Certainly, in her first depression there were chemical issues related to the depression, but my insensitivity to her needs did not help matters. During those years, this attitude only served to increase Trisha's guilt, repressed anger and resentment toward me. If not for a revelation of the Father's love in 1995, we probably would not have made it.

This pattern of myths and mistakes occurs in marriage after marriage and helps fuel the disintegration of the Christian family. Thus, when God moves in powerful ways with a fresh outpouring of His Spirit, we may have deep encounters in His love, but if it does not translate into repentance and application in our marriages, it usually does not bear lasting fruit in our lives, thus revival can be hindered in the church and our nation.

FIVE MARRIAGE SCENARIOS

I share the above mistakes and these scenarios to help you identify where you are in your processing the Father's love. First comes the fulfillment of "the great commandment," then the focus should turn upon "the Great Commission." It has been said that the greatest thing a man can do for his children is to love their mother. I believe that for the hearts of the fathers to be restored to their children, for restoration of the family to begin, for revival to come to our nation, it begins with the restoration of marriages. In many marriages today, the above myths and mistakes result in one of five patterns a wife will follow in response to her husband's inability to meet her emotional needs.

The "no-problem" wife

The "no-problem" wife realizes that her husband is not meeting her emotional needs, but she doesn't know what to do about it. If he asks her if anything is wrong, she typically responds that there is not a problem, but deep inside, she is hoping that someday a miracle will happen and things will change. She is usually a good wife, and she performs her duties well, but while she pours her heart and soul into her marriage, she is not receiving the validation that she needs from her husband, who typically has no idea there is a problem. The "no-problem" wife may unintentionally begin to bond with other men who may give her the sense of value that she is searching for, and the door is opened for an affair to take place.

The "dying inside" or depressed wife

When this wife finds that her husband is not meeting her emotional needs, she may try to deal with the problem at first, but eventually her spirit will begin to wither. These wives often seek help wherever they can find it: in books, in tapes, in church services or counseling. But when no real change takes place, they easily become defeated and may lapse into depression. This wife may lose interest in daily activities and be prone to insomnia or excessive sleep patterns as well as a variety of minor illnesses.

The silent but spiritual wife

My wife is one of the godliest women I know, and I respect her more and more as the years go by. But when we were involved in law and legalism, she mistakenly believed that in order to be spiritual she had to sacrifice her own emotional needs on the altar of my life and ministry. Although outwardly she appeared to be the perfect pastor's wife, inside her emotions were contradicting her actions. She resented me for not meeting her needs, but she felt guilty for resenting me. Our belief systems at that time did not allow her the freedom to express these feelings, so Trisha became "the silent but spiritual wife," never letting her true self be known. Silent but spiritual wives may eventually collapse from the effort of keeping up appearances while denying their true feelings.

The strong-willed wife

These wives are independent, outspoken and not afraid to share what's on their minds. They tend to be received as the nags or criticizers. The criticism is rooted in their own pain and sense of rejection. This type of wife may try to talk to her husband or pastor about her marriage, but her bitterness is often so strong that she is labeled as a troublemaker, or a "Jezebel," in the church. But deep beneath the harsh exterior lies the heart of a wounded little girl who is crying to be loved by the one man who means the most to her, her husband.

The "well, I guess it's not so bad" wife

This is probably the most common type of wife in Christian circles. She thinks to herself, *My life isn't so bad. I've got a good, Christian husband who has a good job, keeps a roof over our heads and seems to love his kids. He may not always meet all of my needs, but at least he doesn't chase after other women or beat me up.* This woman may have all of her physical needs met, but she is still settling for less than God's best. Her husband may say the words, "I love you," but he doesn't understand the heart of a woman. She realizes there is something missing, but she excuses it because he seems to be such a good man.

Each of these five wives can easily begin to wither and dry up inside unless there is a renewal in the marriage, and the heart of the husband turns back to the wife and the heart of the wife turns back to the husband. In our marriage, our commitment to godly values prevented the word *divorce* from ever entering in, but our family was still disintegrating, leaving our children insecure from the instability in the home.

When the revelation of the Father's love broke forth in my heart in November 1995, I was willing to receive it as a move of repentance and revival that was to go beyond the church walls, beyond the acceptance and love that I experienced in renewal meetings. The Father's love is not just about getting our hearts healed and finding the love that we have been searching for all of our life. The Father's love must be processed with humility and repentance being walked out in our families and primary relationships for God's love to bear lasting fruit and before we seek to take it to the world!

RESTORING THE CHRISTIAN FAMILY

In the beginning of this chapter, we saw that God has promised that in the End Times the hearts of the parents will be returned to their children and a restoration of the families of the earth will take place. How does the restoration of the family begin after we have received a personal revelation of the Father's love? How can our marriage be renewed once it has lost its innocence and intimacy? How do we begin to process the Father's love within our family relationships? Please know that your situation may not be resolved overnight, but as you yield to the prompting of the Holy Spirit and cry out to God daily for His grace and love to flow through you to others, you should see healing and restoration begin in your family.

First, restoration begins when we realize that we have been more sensitive to trying to get our needs met than meeting the needs of our family. When we experience the Father's love and begin to see how we have been neglecting the emotional needs of our spouse and children, we will begin to value intimacy more than position, possessions, power or the passions of the flesh. The Word makes it very clear that our primary qualification for leadership in the body of Christ is when our relationship with God is evidenced by our relationship with our family and the degree that we abide in love and intimacy. Ministry to our families must take precedence over our ministry to the world (Matt. 22:37–40; 1 John 4:7–18; Eph. 5:25–33; 1 Pet. 3:1–7; 1 Tim. 3:4–5; 5:8).

When Trisha expressed a legitimate and reasonable need to me, and I did not seek to meet that need, my actions were saying to her that she was last on my list of priorities—everything and everyone were more important to me. It was more important for me to pray for and minister to the people in my church than it was to minister to my family. My wife would watch my ministry at the altar, how gentle and sensitive I could be, and she would cry after we reached home because she never experienced that side of me for herself. For years, I would not even admit there was a problem; I did not realize I was taking my family for granted. I thought that because I was ministering for the Lord and taking care of their physical needs, I deserved their love and praise. But I was not meeting the emotional needs of my family at home. I had been giving too much to others what rightly belonged to my wife and children.

When the Father's love helped me understand that I was lacking in loving my wife as Christ loved the church (Eph. 5:25), and that I did not even know how to start, I had reached the point where change could begin. I saw that my relationship with my family had become mechanical; I had read many books on how to be a good husband and father, but I was performing out of my mind, not releasing a flow of God's love out of my spirit. I began to cry out to God for repentance that was so deep that it would change my behavior and release restoration in my family. I asked Him to help me feel the pain my family did when they felt they had no place in my heart. He gave it to me, and I hardly stopped weeping for the first four months of 1996. (See the chapter on "Walking in the Light.")

Second, the cry of my heart became for God to teach me what it meant to be a husband and father. Being raised in a home where my parents had great conflict and ended in divorce, I had no concept of what a healthy marriage looked like. Having such difficult issues with my father in my youth, I never felt like a son to my father, so how could I be a father until I felt like a son? I knew I must have a deeper personal experience in God's Fatherhood and for His unconditional love to flow through me to my wife and children because I couldn't do it on my own. I had used the excuse for so long that I couldn't give to others what hadn't been given to me. But now God's love was breaking forth in deeper ways, and that excuse would not hold water any longer. The Father had revealed to me, "My child, you have always been with me, and all that is mine is yours" (Luke 15:31). God's love, sensitivity and compassion lie within me, and I am created for my family to experience it through me.

Third, we are to open our heart for God to flow through us and to meet the individual emotional and spiritual needs of our spouse and children. Each individual is different; we have different personalities and understand love in different ways. Because I am a man, I have difficulty understanding the mind of a woman. Now that I am an adult, I find it hard to remember what it was like to be a child or a teenager. So I need to rely on the Holy Spirit to flow through me and to prompt my heart and cause me to be sensitive to the needs of my wife and children. Therefore, several times a day I ask, "Father, show me when I do anything that devalues or brings shame to any member of my family. Show me how to value them in ways that they can understand. Show me how to humble myself to them and to express Your affectionate love." Then I must be willing to do it, no matter how much pride it costs me.

Not long after I began to pray that way, my eighteen-year-old son Micah came into my study to talk to me. I was very busy at the time, working under a deadline, but I waved him in. Not much excites Micah more than playing golf, and this particular day, he couldn't wait to show me his new golf shoes. He had bought them with his own money, and he was beaming as he came around my desk to show them off.

"Look at my shoes, Dad! Aren't they great?" He started to tell me about how his golf game was improving, but his voice began to trail off as he saw my response.

My back was still turned to him while I worked away at my

computer. "Uh, huh, son, that's wonderful," I murmured, and then I heard the door close as he left the room.

My heart dropped. What had I just done to my oldest son? He was sharing the most important part of his life with me, and I couldn't even take the time to turn around and look him in the eye. The conviction of the Holy Spirit weighed heavily upon me, and I jumped up and ran out of my study after him. He had already left, so I called him at the golf course where he worked.

"Micah, I need to apologize. I have misrepresented the Father's love and sinned against you!"

"What did you do, Dad?"

"You were talking about something important to you, but all you saw was the back of my head. I communicated to you that my work in the ministry is more important to me than listening to you. I've sinned against you, and I am asking for your forgiveness."

"Dad, I forgive you. You do it all the time."

My heart was grieved as I realized that my son had become so used to my unresponsiveness that Micah didn't even understand that it was wrong. I may never have had the realization that I had sinned against my son if I had not made a commitment to be sensitive to the Holy Spirit. That event began changing something in me. I started becoming more sensitive to when my children walked into the room. I'm learning to listen to them when they talk to me. I started laying down my agenda and giving them my heart. I ask God each day how I can speak words that will build up their self-esteem. After so many years of emotional neglect and shame, trust began to be rebuilt in my children's heart toward me.

Every day I seek for the Spirit's help in finding ways to help my wife believe that I love her. The words "I love you," while necessary, are not enough if there are not actions to back them up. I'm asking God to give me creative ideas in complimenting Trisha. "Help me to speak her language of affirmation. I don't want to use the same old words. Help me be specific about why I love her and why she looks good today. Father, how can I take Your love and give it away to my wife today?" He is teaching me how to love from her point of view. With the depth of pain that I have known, without a deeper sense of the Father's love and knowing that He is always with me and all that is His is mine, I would not be able to understand or meet the emotional needs of my wife.

HUMILITY IS THE KEY

Trisha wrote the following testimony of the change that has taken place in our family since my first experience in the Father's embrace in November of 1995.

> Over the last seven years, I have watched Jack become more sensitive in the Father's love, and it has brought a whole new life to me. I've seen him become motivated by love rather than by his own selfish needs or ambition. This in turn has motivated me to become all I can be and never to settle for less than the purpose God has created for me.
>
> In the past, when Jack was on the road ministering, there was a sense of heaviness in our home. Not so today. His presence and spirit of love remain in the home through his prayers even when he is gone. The Father has used my husband to pour out His love into me. Now all I want to do is love the Lord and His people because Jack's unconditional love has motivated me to do so. Even our own children are being influenced by Jack's love and compassion to become more like the Father.
>
> I have done a lot of repenting myself lately for not fully trusting Jack. Even though he has changed so much, I still treat him like the old Jack at times. I am learning how to rest in his love, and my love for him continues to grow as I see the Father's love in him.
>
> Our family is now living one of the most exciting lives on earth as we seek to give the Father's love away every moment of each day to one another with an overflowing love.

This type of change in our household was only able to take place when I made a conscious determination to relinquish my pride and seek the humility of Christ. My pride had caused me to place my career, my goals and my ministry ahead of the needs of my family, but when I began to humble myself and realize that I was created for love and making it known to my family first and the nations second, that is when the process of restoration began. My relationship with Trisha was not only renewed, but it also became sweeter and more intimate than I had ever believed possible. When our marriage moved into deeper depths of intimacy, the children became more secure in themselves and in the family, and their lives began to blossom. And ironically, the shift in my priorities was not detrimental to our ministry in any way—in fact, the anointing of God has fallen on us in an even stronger sense, and we now have invitations to minister all over the world.

Are you willing to receive the spirit of Christ (humility) in your family? In the power of the Father's love, are you willing to empty yourself of all of your selfish ambitions and desires and take on the form of a servant in your home? Are you willing to take up the cross daily for your spouse and your children? When you do that, you begin to become an instrument of the Father's love, and restoration begins in your family.

God wants to bring each of us to a new understanding of His love. The Father longs to gather His children in His arms; He craves the relationship of love and intimacy with you for which He created you. Your life will never be more fulfilled than when you follow His lifestyle of love, asking Him each day, "Father, help me to experience Your affectionate love and then pass it along to the next person I meet." God desires a revival to sweep the land— a fresh revival of His love to touch every human being. He promises restoration of our hearts, lives and families when we turn to Him and experience the Father's embrace.

QUESTIONS FOR DISCUSSION

1. If you are married, evaluate your relationship with your spouse. From the list of sixteen mistakes commonly made in marriage, talk about the mistakes you feel you have made in your marriage.

2. Why is it so important for a married couple to be open about their deepest emotions? How do you feel you could improve emotional intimacy in your marriage?

3. If you have children, share how you could improve communication and intimacy with them.

Conclusion

> Everyone who loves is born of God and experiences a relationship with God. The person who refuses to love doesn't know the first thing about God, because God is love—so you can't know him if you don't love...God is love. When we take up permanent residence in a life of love, we live in God and God lives in us. This way, love has the run of the house, becomes at home and mature in us...We, though, are going to love—love and be loved. First we were loved, now we love. He loved us first.
>
> —1 JOHN 4:7–8, 16, 19, THE MESSAGE

These verses imply that true love for God must stand the daily test of my life with others. I have never been more aware how little of the Father's love I have really experienced. It can best be measured by my everyday interactions with people and the love, or lack of it, I display. The thing that often holds me back from deeper experiences and revelation in the Father's affectionate embrace is the great struggle I face daily between pride and humility. There are two master powers, two kingdoms, battling within me for the dominating influence of my life: the kingdom of pride and the kingdom of humility. I don't know about you, but I am personally aware of pride winning some battles far too often. Jesus' words to His disciples at the Last Supper help to reveal this in me.

> And there arose also a dispute among them as to which one of them was regarded to be greatest..."Let him who is the greatest among you become as the youngest, and the leader as the servant. For who is greater, the one who reclines at the

table, or the one who serves? Is it not the one who reclines
at the table? But I am among you as the one who serves.

—LUKE 22:24, 26–27

The more success, honor and position that I am receiving in
ministry, the more I catch myself gravitating toward wanting my
family and others to serve me. I say to myself, "Look at how God
is using me! Everyone ought to be quick to jump on board and
help me so I can run to the world with the Father's love!" That
kind of thinking is contrary to the life of Christ and His walk in
love.

Deep down in my soul, there seems to be a darkness of which
I sometimes am hardly aware. I've attained a measure of God's
grace and love; yet, like the disciples at the Last Supper, too often
something in me still seeks the place of honor more than the
lower place. If I am truly looking to lead my family and others
into a revelation of the Father's love, I will not lead from a position of being over them, but from being beneath them. Jesus is
the proof of that!

> Have this attitude in yourselves which was also in Christ
> Jesus, who, although He existed in the form of God, did not
> regard equality with God a thing to be grasped, but emptied
> Himself, taking the form of a bond-servant, and being made
> in the likeness of men.
>
> —PHILIPPIANS 2:5–7

Like Jesus, a true servant-leader is devoted to the needs and
interests of those he leads. He gives careful thought and study as
to how he can minister to others more than they to him. He
delights in helping others be promoted, honored and happy. He
lives to see others mature and become all they can be in the kingdom of love. "He must increase, but I must decrease" (John 3:30).
Oh, how I realize that far too often this is not the way my thinking goes.

Once the revelation of the Father's sacrificial love becomes true revelation to me, I am to embrace more fully humility and the spirit of servanthood with my family and others, even with those difficult people I have in my life. Only then will others truly experience the Father's love through me, and only then will I be released to manifest the Father's love to the world. The lowest place is where the river of God's love flows best. Water always seeks the lowest place. The lower I humble myself before others, the deeper the revelation of the Father's love, power and glory will be seen by others in me. That is what humility is: recognizing my inability to do anything without God's ability (grace) daily filling my emptiness. This is what most effectively releases God's love flowing through me to others, not my ability to handle the anointing or to teach the Word of God.

I have found a pattern I often seem to follow in the dealings of God that I experience in my pursuit to dwell in the Father's embrace.

First, my response to being humbled by God's love is not usually good. I tend to run from the things that give me an opportunity to humble myself and to walk in God's love—things like seeking forgiveness and reconciliation from each person with whom I have or have had unresolved issues. I do not apologize so quickly to family when I've misrepresented the Father's love or sought my own desires more than theirs. I find it so easy to center conversations around me and the things that bring me pleasure. I do not always find myself seeking to honor and promote others' ministries as I desire to do my own. It is evident that, though I long for humility, I see no value in humiliations. Therefore, I have not yet learned to seek it at any cost. I do not let my self-love sell out to humility.

Second, I begin to experience a sense of grief as I realize that humility is not a joy and pleasure to me. I begin to realize that I have moved off center of walking in the Father's love and moved into aggressively striving for the higher place. Paul found pleasure and glory in his weaknesses and humiliations. He knew humility to be the place of love, blessing and power.

> And He has said to me, "My grace is sufficient for you, for power is perfected in weakness." Most gladly, therefore, I will rather boast about my weaknesses, that the power of Christ may dwell in me. Therefore I am well content with weaknesses, with insults, with distresses, with persecutions, with difficulties, for Christ's sake; for when I am weak, then I am strong.
>
> —2 CORINTHIANS 12:9–10

I realize that when someone is making life difficult for me, I do not take pleasure in the things that bring me low, and it takes far too long for me to become aware of my need for deeper humility and love.

Third, I start feeling the pain my family and others feel from the devaluing I bring to them when they know my personal agenda is more important than relationship with them. The grief I feel over my pride (need to be right) and misrepresentations of the Father's love begins to lead me into deeper repentance. I start crying out for greater revelation of God's grace within me. It is only my daily surrendering to the Father's love that can expel the self-love with which I struggle.

Fourth, after fresh revelation, I begin to make new choices to humble myself before my family and others. I now see each act of humility as a source of deeper experience in God's love, blessing and power. This is what exalts me into the Father's presence where His loving nature begins to dispel layers of pride, resulting in deeper humility and acts of service and love to others.

> And do not be called leaders; for One is your Leader, that is Christ. But the greatest among you shall be your servant. And whoever exalts himself shall be humbled; and whoever humbles himself shall be exalted.
>
> —MATTHEW 23:10–11

These verses release in me a key to conquering pride and experiencing the Father's embrace: I am to humble myself. Every act of humility before man destroys the workings of pride in my heart! Every time I am hurt, disappointed by someone or humiliated before man, I let this remind me of my desperate need for a deeper revelation of Christ's love and grace through His humility being released in me. It is not my work to conquer pride. It is my work to humble myself at every opportunity before man.

Many times I seek to conquer pride in the flesh and not by the Spirit. This leads to patterns of shame and guilt. I begin to see how deeply pride runs throughout my motives, attitudes and actions. I get into self-condemnation. I get tired of the heaviness and try to break pride's hold by the letter of the law. "*I must* be humble! *I must* repent!" But my flesh is unwilling to submit to humbling myself before man. There is too much "*I must*" and not enough "*I want* more of Christ's humility and love released in my character!" I end up realizing how helpless I am and how much pride consumes me. Then aggressive striving and hyperreligious activity increases! I have followed this pattern many times.

Andrew Murray's book *Humility* has helped me see how impossible it is for me to cast out pride. It was pride that brought self-seeking desires (sin) to the earth. Pride, the lack of humility, is the root of everything that is contrary to the Father's love. Only humility can expel pride in me. You do not cast out the darkness; you turn on the light, and the light dispels the darkness. I need only do what God asks: at every opportunity, commit myself to loving acts of humility before my family and others. Then God will do the thing He has promised: He will exalt me, in due season, into deeper depths of His humility and love. It can never be a performance thing. It is the positioning of our heart by entering into the lowly place.

ACTS
(Humbling myself before family and others...)

PRODUCE HABITS
(I begin to see others as God's creation,
preferring them above myself.)

HABITS BREED ATTITUDES
(I begin to find pleasure in acts of humility.)

ATTITUDES STRENGTHEN
AND FORM MY WILL
(I trust God to do the work of defending,
honoring and exalting me.)

WILL DEVELOPS MY CHARACTER
(Grace [God's ability], love and humility increase as I am
exalted into God's presence, where the humility of Christ
displaces pride within me.)

Humility is to be the truest characteristic of my life in Christ and my experience in the Father's love. "Take My yoke upon you, and learn from Me, for I am gentle and humble in heart; and you shall find rest for your souls" (Matt. 11:29).

Humility before my family and others is the only sufficient proof of my humility before God! This is the key that unlocks deeper depths of experience in the Father's embrace. Therefore, I am seeking to make the chief pursuit of my life, the Father's love that is rooted in humility. I do know one thing: I will certainly be tested in this every day for the rest of my life!

Your family and a lost and hurting world are waiting for you to join Christ in the Father's mission—to experience His love and give it away to the next person you meet.

> In the same way that you gave me a mission in the world, I give them a mission in the world...The goal is for all of them to become one heart and mind—just as you, Father, are in me and I in you, so they might be one heart and mind with us. Then the world might believe that you, in fact, sent me. The same glory you gave me, I gave them, so they'll be as unified and together as we are—I in them and you in me. Then they'll be mature in this oneness, and give the godless world evidence that you've sent me and loved them in the same way you've loved me.
>
> —JOHN 17:18, 21–23, THE MESSAGE

The Father's Love Letter: The Cry of a Father's Heart From Genesis to Revelation

My child...

You may not know Me, but I know everything about you...
Psalm 139:1

I know when you sit down and when you rise up...Psalm
139:2

I am familiar with all your ways...Psalm 139:3

Even the very hairs on your head are numbered...Matthew
10:29–31

For you were made in My image...Genesis 1:27

In Me you live and move and have your being...Acts 17:28

For you are My offspring...Acts 17:28

I knew you even before you were conceived...Jeremiah
1:4–5

I chose you when I planned creation...Ephesians 1:11–12

You were not a mistake, for all your days are written in My
book...Psalm 139:15–16

I determined the exact time of your birth and where you
would live...Acts 17:26

You are fearfully and wonderfully made...Psalm 139:14

I knit you together in your mother's womb...Psalm 139:13

And brought you forth on the day you were born...Psalm
71:6

I have been misrepresented by those who don't know Me...
John 8:41–44

I am not distant and angry, but am the complete expression
of love...1 John 4:16

And it is My desire to lavish My love on you...1 John 3:1

Simply because you are My child and I am your father...1
John 3:1

I offer you more than your earthly father ever could...
Matthew 7:11

For I am the perfect father...Matthew 5:48

Every good gift that you receive comes from My hand...
James 1:17

For I am your provider, and I meet all your needs...
Matthew 6:31–33

My plan for your future has always been filled with hope...
Jeremiah 29:11

Because I love you with an everlasting love...Jeremiah 31:3

My thoughts toward you are countless as the sand on the
seashore...Psalm 139:17–18

And I rejoice over you with singing...Zephaniah 3:17

I will never stop doing good to you...Jeremiah 32:40

For you are My treasured possession...Exodus 19:5

I desire to establish you with all My heart and all My soul...
Jeremiah 32:41

And I want to show you great and marvelous things...
Jeremiah 33:3

If you seek Me with all your heart, you will find Me...
Deuteronomy 4:29

Delight in Me, and I will give you the desires of your heart...
Psalm 37:4

For it is I who gave you those desires...Philippians 2:13

I am able to do more for you than you could possibly
imagine...Ephesians 3:20

For I am your greatest encourager...2 Thessalonians
2:16–17

I am also the Father who comforts you in all your

troubles…2 Corinthians 1:3–4

When you are brokenhearted, I am close to you…Psalm 34:18

As a shepherd carries a lamb, I have carried you close to My heart…Isaiah 40:11

One day I will wipe away every tear from your eyes… Revelation 21:3–4

And I'll take away all the pain you have suffered on this earth…Revelation 21:3–4

I am your Father, and I love you even as I love My son, Jesus…John 17:23

For in Jesus, My love for you is revealed…John 17:26

He is the exact representation of My being…Hebrews 1:3

He came to demonstrate that I am for you, not against you…Romans 8:31

And to tell you that I am not counting your sins… 2 Corinthians 5:18–19

Jesus died so that you and I could be reconciled… 2 Corinthians 5:18–19

His death was the ultimate expression of My love for you…1 John 4:10

I gave up everything I loved that I might gain your love… Romans 8:31–32

If you receive the gift of My Son, Jesus, you receive me… 1 John 2:23

And nothing will ever separate you from My love again… Romans 8:38–39

Come home, and I'll throw the biggest party heaven has ever seen…Luke 15:7

I have always been Father and will always be Father… Ephesians 3:14–15

My question is…Will you be My child?…John 1:12–13

I am waiting for you…Luke 15:11–32

Love, Your Dad, Almighty God[1]

You can order the thirty-minute video *The Father's Love Letter* or an audio version from Shiloh Place Ministries. These can be previewed on our website www.shilohplace.org or ordered from:

Shiloh Place Ministries
P. O. Box 5
Conway, SC 29526
(843) 365-8990

Notes

CHAPTER 2: YOU WERE CREATED FOR LOVE

1. Dean Ornish, M.D., *Love and Survival: The Scientific Basis for the Healing Power of Intimacy* (New York: HarperCollins Publishers, Inc., 1998).

CHAPTER 4: THE PRODIGAL FATHER

1. *Webster's Ninth New Collegiate Dictionary* (Springfield, MA: Merriam-Webster, Inc., 1991), s.v. "prodigal."

2. Source obtained from the Internet: "Laymen: Motivated to Honor and Ministry," an interview with Bill McCartney, *Enrichment Journal* (Fall 1998): http://enrichmentjournal. ag.org/enrichmentjournal/199804/042_laymen.cfm. Accessed July 9, 2002.

3. The information for the acrostic FIG LEAF is adapted from Carroll Thompson, *The Bruises of Satan* (Dallas: Christ for the Nations, 1982).

CHAPTER 5: THE OLDER BROTHER SYNDROME, OR THE SON WILLING TO BECOME A SLAVE

1. Jack Winter, *The Homecoming* (Seattle, WA: YWAM Publishers, 1999).

CHAPTER 6: DEALING WITH FATHER ISSUES

1. Source obtained from the Internet: Chuck Baldwin, "As Pulpit Goes, So Goes Nation," *The Covenant News* (July 10, 2001): www.covenantnews.com/baldwin070710.htm. Accessed July 10, 2002.

CHAPTER 7: DEALING WITH MOTHER ISSUES

1. Thomas R. Verny, *Secret Life of the Unborn Child* (New York: Dell Publishing Co., 1994).

CHAPTER 9: WALKING IN THE LIGHT

1. Roy Hession, *The Calvary Road* (Fort Washington, PA: Christian Literature Crusade, 1980).

CHAPTER 10: ABIDING IN LOVE

1. Norman P. Grubb, *Continuous Revival* (Fort Washington, PA: Christian Literature Crusade, 1997).

CHAPTER 12: RESTORING THE HEART OF THE FAMILY

1. Source obtained from the Internet: World Divorce Statistics, *Divorce Magazine,* www.divorcemag.com/statistics/statsWorld. Accessed July 15, 2002.

2. Source obtained from the Internet: Family, Barna Research Online, www.barna.org. Accessed July 15, 2002.

3. Ken Nair, *Discovering the Mind of a Woman* (Nashville: Thomas Nelson, 1995).

AFTERWORD: THE FATHER'S LOVE LETTER

1. Barry Adams, "The Father's Love Letter," copyright © 1999 Father Heart Communications, www.FathersLoveLetter.com. Used by permission.

RESOURCES TO HELP YOU EXPERIENCE THE FATHER'S EMBRACE

RESTORING THE FATHER'S LOVE (5-audiotape series)

God has placed within each of us a desire to experience our parents' love and to find a place of comfort and protection in their hearts. Because parents could not perfectly meet our needs, we often grow up insecure with intimacy and love. We end up spending our lives looking for love in all the wrong ways, and we begin striving to impress God, others or ourselves. This series will help to identify hidden core pain from our parents' house and begin to restore many to the love they have been longing for all of their lives.

YOU WERE CREATED FOR LOVE (4-audiotape series)

When God created you, He programmed every fiber of your being for love and intimacy. There is nothing more natural than for you to be "a lover" and to walk in healthy, loving relationships that are free from fear, control and feelings of separation. "While I was on vacation, my girlfriend and I listened to this series while we were driving. I have heard much teaching on the love of the Father, but while listening to these tapes, I felt such a depth stirred! So here we were, driving on the motorway, traveling in the fast lane with the convertible top down, blasting your tapes and tears were flowing down our cheeks (it's a good thing we were wearing our sunglasses). Thanks for the wonderful resource you've provided." Petra in Toronto

HINDRANCES TO RECEIVING THE FATHER'S LOVE (4-audiotape series)

No matter how much your earthly parents provided for your physical needs, if you did not feel safe and secure in their hearts, you may spend your entire life looking for a home, a place of comfort and rest. This leaves many Christians feeling like spiritual orphans who find it difficult to find intimacy and rest in God. Therefore, they slowly drift either toward aggressive striving and hyperreligious activity or toward fleshly indulgences or addictions. This series helps to identify some root causes to the things that separate us from deep intimacy with God and man. As you listen, be prepared to enter into some deep depths of repentance and experience a homecoming in Father's affectionate embrace.

PROCESSING THE FATHER'S LOVE (4-audiotape series)

The abiding sense of the Father's loving embrace and the healing of our souls are not just experiences that come with dramatic encounters. They are processes that are daily walked out through our daily choices and interactions in everyday relationships. When Christ died on the cross and we accepted Him in our hearts, we received all the love of God that we will receive for all eternity in our spirit man. Our spirits have been perfected in His love. In this series, you will learn how it is possible to abide daily in the Spirit through moment-by-moment acts of humility and love. This understanding is a must as we begin to pursue deeper depths of God's love!

FROM SLAVERY TO SONSHIP (3-audiotape series)

Each of us was created with a capacity to receive love from a mother and father. Yet, many of us cannot say that we have behaved as true sons or daughters to our parents or to our spiritual fathers. When we rejected the "spirit of sonship" (a spirit of submission), as teenagers we took on an attitude of independence or self-reliance, taking control of our lives. This can easily later overflow into our relationship with authority and Father God. This series addresses the issues of feeling like spiritual orphans (like we have never had a safe or secure home), receiving our inheritance in Christ and entering into true intimacy with God, spiritual authority and others.

THE PRAYER MINISTRY OF THE FATHER'S LOVE (4-audiotape series)

Jack becomes very transparent in order to equip you to minister the Father's healing love to another person through healing prayer. In every word you'll find Father God reaching out to embrace a wounded child. As you allow God to use your loving arms and your encouraging words of love and forgiveness, you'll find your own life has changed as well.

HEALING PRAYERS FOR THE SOUL (3-audiotape series)
Great for waiting in God's presence and allowing Him to love on you! This series contains prayers often prayed during corporate ministry times at the conclusion of Jack's conferences. Prayers for forgiving fathers and mothers, confession of sin, repentance, giving and receiving forgiveness, pulling down mental and demonic strongholds, renouncing ungodly beliefs, cleansing of shame and sexual defilements, healing for emotional and physical pain, and receiving a deeper experience in the Father's loving embrace are offered. Recorded live at a major conference, the sounds of music, praying and weeping can be heard in the background as Jack leads the group in this powerful time of entering into the Father's embrace.

These resources, gentle music about the Father's love and other teaching videos and manuals by Jack Frost that will help you experience healing in your family relationships and intimacy with God, can be ordered through our secured website at www.shilohplace.org, or you may contact:

Shiloh Place Ministries
P. O. Box 5
Conway, SC 29528
(843) 365-8990